Investigation Centers

Open Minds to Expand and Improve God's Kingdom

Donald Mitchell

Author of *Your Breakthroughs,*
2,000 Percent Living, and *Excellent Solutions*
Coauthor of *The 2,000 Percent Solution*

400 Year Project Press
Weston, Massachusetts
United States of America

400 Year Project Books by Donald Mitchell

Your Breakthroughs

2,000 Percent Living
Help Wanted

Excellent Solutions (For-Profit and Nonprofit Editions)
Excellent Leadership

The 2,000 Percent Nation

Witnessing Made Easy (with Bishop Dale Combs, Lisa Combs, Jim Barbarossa, and Carla Barbarossa)
Ways You Can Witness (with Cherie Hill, Roger de Brabant, Drew Dickens, Gael Torcise, Wendy Lobos, Herpha Jane Obod, and Gisele Umugiraneza)

The 2,000 Percent Solution (with Carol Coles and Robert Metz)
The Portable 2,000 Percent Solution (with Carol Coles)
The 2,000 Percent Solution Workbook (with Carol Coles)
The 2,000 Percent Squared Solution (with Carol Coles)

The Irresistible Growth Enterprise (with Carol Coles)
The Ultimate Competitive Advantage (with Carol Coles)

Business Basics

Advanced Business
Advanced Business for Innovation
Advanced Business for Social Benefits

Adventures of an Optimist

Investigation Centers
Open Minds to Expand and Improve God's Kingdom

ISBN: 978-0692716885
0692716882

For information, contact:

Donald W. Mitchell
400 Year Project Press
P.O. Box 302
Weston, Massachusetts 02493
781-647-4211

Published in the United States of America

This book is dedicated to:

Expanders and improvers of God's Kingdom
who apply The 400 Year Project's
and other breakthrough methods

May quickly and easily making Godly breakthroughs
always be ahead of them!

And their spouses, their children and grandchildren,
and their descendants

May this book help them to always focus
on the Lord and doing His will!

Contents

Acknowledgments

Oh, give thanks to the LORD!
Call upon His name;
Make known His deeds among the peoples!

— 1 Chronicles 16:8 (NKJV)

I thank Almighty God, our Heavenly Father, for creating the universe and all the people on the Earth; our Lord and Savior, Jesus Christ, for providing the way for us to gain Salvation; and the Holy Spirit for guiding our daily paths towards repentance and righteousness. I also humbly acknowledge the perfect guidance I was sent from God through the Holy Spirit and His Word to write this book. I regret that as an imperfect being I undoubtedly misheard, misunderstood, and misapplied some of that perfect guidance.

I feel deeply honored by Pastor Doug Whallon writing the book's excellent foreword. His decades of experience with adult discipleship have been a powerful source of wisdom for me in my spiritual development both as a learner and as a teacher. In the early days of the writing, he provided excellent direction for possible models to consider. While he is a great pastor to me and many others, I also consider him to be a wonderful friend. I could not be more blessed in both of these ways.

I am grateful to Peter Drucker for encouraging me to write about 2,000 percent solutions (ways of accomplishing 20 times more with the same or less time, effort, and resources) and to seek ever-simpler ways to help people learn to employ them. His faith in this method for solving problems caused me to take much more seriously the opportunity to share what I had been doing.

I appreciate all those who have permitted me to tell them about 2,000 percent solution methods and the output of The 400 Year Project in improving far beyond these methods. I thank those who have applied what they learned for all the insights I have gained from observing their wonderful work.

I can never thank my family enough for allowing me the time and peace to engage in such a large and awe-inspiring project for God. They made many sacrifices without complaining and have been a continual inspiration.

I appreciate my many clients who held off on their demands for my help so that this project could receive the attention it required. Their financial support also made it possible for me to give this time to the Lord and to make this book available.

Finally, I am most appreciative of the many fine improvements that my editor, Bernice Pettinato, made in the text. This is the twentieth book for which she has helped me to make the messages clearer and more pleasant to read. As always, she was a delight to work with. Her kindness made the writing much easier. I value all she has taught me about writing. I look forward to learning new lessons from her during future books.

I accept sole responsibility for any remaining errors and apologize to my readers for any difficulties and inconvenience that they encounter as a consequence.

Foreword

Then Jesus answered and said:
"A certain man *went down from Jerusalem to Jericho,*
and fell among thieves, who stripped him of his clothing,
wounded him, *and departed, leaving* him *half dead.*

Now by chance a certain priest came down that road.
And when he saw him, he passed by on the other side.

Likewise a Levite, when he arrived at the place,
came and looked, and passed by on the other side.

But a certain Samaritan, as he journeyed, came where he was.
And when he saw him, he had compassion.

So he went to him *and bandaged his wounds,*
pouring on oil and wine; and he set him on his own animal,
brought him to an inn, and took care of him.

On the next day, when he departed, he took out two denarii,
gave them *to the innkeeper, and said to him,*
'Take care of him; and whatever more you spend,
when I come again, I will repay you.'

So which of these three do you think was neighbor
to him who fell among the thieves?"

And he said, "He who showed mercy on him."

Then Jesus said to him, "Go and do likewise."

— Luke 10:30-37 (NKJV)

What do you do when you have an itch? Most of us give the itch a good scratch. Sometimes other resources are needed, such as a medicating cream or a back scratcher or a friend. But doing nothing is not likely to be the solution.

So, what do you do when you have a mental or emotional itch? It doesn't have to be of gigantic, inscrutable, philosophic proportions — though it could be. There are more common, everyday concerns or issues that almost any thinking person might have. For instance, you might be itching about very practical things, such as what to do for a job, where to live, whom to befriend, what to do with your spare time, or how to invest your money. Or you may be wondering about various relationship itches, such as how to build healthy, resilient long-term friendships, or how to repair old ones that have turned sour or self-destructed. Or you may be deeply concerned about the larger, framework type of questions, such as what makes life worth living, or how to handle your hopes and disappointments, or what it means to live in community or how to best address the world's devastating problems. These are all questions and concerns well worth pursuing. Doing nothing is simply not going to be healthy or smart. For your sake or for the world's, please pay attention to your itches.

So where does one turn? Wikipedia? The neighborhood public library? Go back to college? Any of those might be helpful — but only in a limited way. Alternatively, in the lessons ahead, Don Mitchell introduces us to a range of ideas and possibilities. He takes the time to raise the challenges and analyze some of the problems. In doing so, he guides us along a pathway toward possible solutions. In particular, Don identifies key qualities and attributes that can be packaged together in what he terms "investigation centers."

Our author's "investigation centers" could seem to some to be idealized, imaginary utopias. Perhaps, the charge might be made that he is suggesting something that is "if you can build it, then people will come to it — and be forever changed." Actually, I don't think that is his basic premise. Rather, Don helps us (those who might have potential to take the initiative in developing these kind of places) to empathize with those who may have a whole range of unmet, pressing needs. Those needs range from serious misunderstandings, to loneliness, to emotional and physical burdens, to existential lostness. Then, Don explains how we can become more responsive, respectful, and even healing people — while providing discerning presence, hospitality, and loving assistance. What a joy it is to take other people and their itches or questions or problems seriously. What a privilege to be there for them, recognizing their uniqueness and potential.

In Luke 10:25-37 (NKJV), we can read the story Jesus told of the Good Samaritan who journeyed a roadway, finding a victim whose injuries were far worse than most itches. The Good Samaritan tended to and then transported the injured man to an inn. By way of a loose analogy, I'd suggest that Don's investigation centers are like the inn and its owner. It's both a place and a set of sensitive, compassionate responders who serve those who enter. And the benefits may be temporal or eternal or both.

I am not sure how many investigation centers will be built. The more the better — the world will be a better, safer, kinder, helping place. But do understand that Don realizes that the essence of these centers will take various forms, as circumstances and resources permit. This book offers a clear vision, but the spirit of it embraces flexible delivery systems.

Having said that, I want to suggest that if you want to see a "real live" investigation center, you arrange a meeting with Don Mitchell (just "askdonmitchell@yahoo.com"), as he personifies the kind of place he recommends. His lifestyle and personal approach show me that this "really can get done." With that in mind, I also suggest that Don's design for investigation centers be viewed as equally applicable to a vibrant church, or an engaging small group, or a healthy family home. So, as you read this, may you aspire to either build this kind of investigation center, or to embody these qualities in who you are. For the glory of God.

Doug Whallon
Bedford, Massachusetts
May, 2016

Introduction

"And whoever will not receive you nor hear your words,
when you depart from that house or city,
shake off the dust from your feet."

— Matthew 10:14 (NKJV)

In Jesus' instructions for sharing the Gospel, the disciples were directed to focus on those who were open to receiving them and hearing from them about expanding and improving God's Kingdom. While I would like to be able to say that I've always been receiving and immediately acting on God's directions, I must begin this book with a confession: God has been telling me for several years to write a book encouraging the establishment of investigation centers (a variety of appealing places where questions about God's Kingdom and other important matters are pleasantly and meaningfully answered), but I kept putting off the task. I apologize to God and to you, my reader, for this delay. While I have no excuse for having waited so long, the good news is that I now feel full of the Holy Spirit's wisdom about what to share with you. I'm glad that God didn't give up on me, so that you now hold in your hands this book about such investigation centers. I pray that these contents will bless you and lead you to contribute towards establishing and operating investigation centers that will help draw many people closer to the Lord.

When God prepares me for a task, He usually begins by causing me to notice some things that bother me. I believe that such experiences are designed to help me explain His purposes to readers. In the case of investigation centers, I have long been bothered in two ways that continue to grate on me.

First, I *never* see a church building that I feel drawn to enter. Instead, seeing church buildings instills the opposite reaction: I want to avoid going in. Why? To me, church buildings more often resemble fortresses staffed by people fighting off invaders than they do places where people are looking to know and help me. Even when I have been attending a church for several years and always experienced warm fellowship, worship, and learning with other believers there, I have to gird myself to overcome this reaction before entering the building.

Second, I live in an area near where the Christian Science faith originated, and such churches are somewhat common here. Christian Science churches often locate "reading rooms" near, but not in, their sanctuary buildings. Every time I pass such a reading facility, I wonder what it is supposed to be used for. Part of that puzzlement is due to rarely having seen anyone in the rooms, except the occasional person straightening up. So even when I pass such a reading room on the coldest day in winter and would love a temporary warm up anywhere indoors, I'm never tempted to enter one and learn more.

I'm sure that you join me in being struck by the obvious irony: Those who attend a church, as well as the leaders of churches that provide reading rooms, intend that people will be drawn to and visit them. Is my reaction to such facilities unique? I do not think so. When our church hosts a "fun" day for families in our community, some people who attend tell us that they have never been in a church before. One of my grandfathers always lived near churches, yet he never attended one. My mother and I would visit him after services on Sundays, and he would react to our invitations to join us in attending there by laughing at the idea.

You may be wondering how I overcome my adverse reactions to seeing church buildings to actually enter one for the first time. Usually, someone I know well and respect has told me that those who teach and worship in a given church are well worth knowing and hearing. I also pray about the accuracy of the advice and listen to what the Holy Spirit reveals. Invariably, I find such advice to be true. In a few cases where pastors have shared their sermons on the radio, online, or on television, I have listened to get a sense of what it will be like inside and then decided to enter. Sometimes God takes a hand by being more direct, such as by seating me in a vehicle driven by someone who takes me to a church without first asking me if I want to go.

God called me to attend a different church about four years ago. While the change has been a good one in every way except for missing Sundays with people I like at my former church, I still found virtually every aspect of shifting churches to be awkward, uncomfortable, and difficult. All of that turbulence is behind me now, but the memory is fresh enough that I can still empathize with those who might feel awkward about entering a church to find answers to their questions about God, life, and their problems. This book is designed to help create places where such people will, instead, be eager to enter, joyfully learn, and make good use of such answers.

Why might God have wanted this book to be written and read? Well, He knows and I do not. Perhaps we will find out in heaven. However, I can see some possibilities that you might consider. First, people who want to know more about God, but aren't attending a church, could find an investigation center to be a help. When that happens, God's Kingdom may be expanded by someone eventually becoming a believer. Second, some churches don't do much to deepen believers' knowledge of and relationships with God. For those who attend such churches, investigation centers may play a role in maturing disciples who then more effectively and often help to expand and improve God's Kingdom. Third, God might use investigation centers to encourage good works by creating awareness of appealing opportunities to serve others, thus inspiring some nonbelievers to learn more about such service and possibly become interested in the motivations that inspire those who do so. Fourth, believers may have practical problems that their churches aren't focused on, and an investigation center could provide the only alternative to secular programs that oppose God's purposes. Fifth, while almost all communities have places where information can be shared, in the United States and some other countries public facilities are often denied to those who want to discuss spiritual issues. Although there may be "free speech" in such countries, few are going to hear about spiritual matters unless some money is spent to provide a venue and attract an audience. Sixth, in most communities there is no place where someone can learn the breakthrough methods of The 400 Year Project, and investigation centers may be part of God's plan for encouraging the use of these methods. The Holy Spirit may reveal other possibilities to you for why God wants investigation centers to be established. Keep those possibilities in mind as you read this book: Perhaps God is calling you to implement such a benefit.

Investigation Centers: Open Minds to Expand and Improve God's Kingdom is divided into four parts. In Part One, we consider unmet needs that might be served by investigation centers. Each of seven unmet needs is addressed in a separate lesson. If you think of any unmet needs not covered in Part One, I encourage you to share them with me at donmitchell@fastforward400.com/. In Part Two, we shift to considering eight qualities an investigation center should have to best serve the unmet needs that are discussed in Part One. While each quality is addressed in a separate lesson, an investigation center should obviously seek to supply all of these qualities to those who would benefit. Part Three addresses eight possible models for supplying the desirable qualities covered in Part Two, with each model considered in a separate lesson. Finally, in Part Four, I describe ways that such individual models might best be combined and improved in light of local needs and circumstances. You will also find my personal testimony in Appendix A. You might find reading about my experiences with God will help you to seek and hear Him better. In Appendix B, I briefly summarize The 400 Year Project, the 20-year effort from 1995 to 2015 that developed many breakthrough-improvement methods that can be used to engage in the investigation-center opportunities described in Part Four.

If you have any questions or comments about investigation centers or this book, I welcome your e-mails directed to me. You can reach me at donmitchell@fastforward400.com/.

Part One:

Unmet Needs

"Therefore do not worry, saying,
'What shall we eat?' or 'What shall we drink?' or
'What shall we wear?'
For after all these things the Gentiles seek.
For your heavenly Father knows that you need all these things.
But seek first the kingdom of God and His righteousness,
and all these things shall be added to you."

— Matthew 6:31-33 (NKJV)

While God aims to supply all the unmet needs to those in His Kingdom, a much more limited portion will be directly supplied through investigation centers. However, an investigation center's role in this regard may be wider than you think. While some might assume that investigation centers are only for those who don't yet have a relationship with our Savior, Jesus Christ, I believe that attending such centers will often improve and deepen relationships with God for believers, especially for those who have not received much support for sanctification (becoming more like Jesus). After you finish reading Part One, I'm sure you'll understand why I say so.

Since the subject of what needs investigation centers should serve is undoubtedly new to you, to help orient you here's an overview of the Part One lessons. In Lesson One, we consider how to correct misunderstandings. Many people know too little about God's Kingdom to accurately understand and appreciate what the Kingdom is. In other cases, people have imagined God as being who they do or do not want Him to be, rather than who He actually is. Some other people have also had painful experiences with believers, experiences that have caused misunderstandings about what God wants us to be like and to do.

Lesson Two explores answering questions that almost everyone has. From this perspective, it is easier to appreciate the potential of investigation centers in informing believers. For any such individuals who do not attend church, do not study the Bible, or attend a church where they find it difficult to ask and receive meaningful answers, the list of questions may be quite long: Why do bad things happen to "good" people? Where do people go after they die? Why should someone be baptized? What difference can attending church make? When will God answer my prayers? What is my calling? As you can see, the first two questions will also be in the minds of many nonbelievers, and the remaining questions will be asked by many believers.

In Lesson Three, we discuss a common need for nonbelievers and believers alike: satisfying curiosity. For instance, someone who doesn't know any believers may want to understand a little about the Christian faith. A believer might want to hear about experiences other believers have had that increased and rewarded their faith. Everyone might have curiosity about what people of faith think about faith-denying comments made by doubters.

Lesson Four deals with one of my own issues: overcoming discomfort. However, I suspect that fear of discomfort influences the behavior of almost everyone at least a little. In my many years serving as a church usher, for instance, I never remember being asked by a first-time visitor for a seat in the front row. Instead, any row other than the last one in back usually seemed too close for comfort. Those who don't want to be "preached at," challenged to do something they don't want to do, "talked down to," or given too much attention need some place to go where it's obviously unlikely they will experience such forms of discomfort.

In Lesson Five, we see the opposite circumstance: someone wanting, but lacking, enough friendly fellowship. Over the last two centuries, fiction writers and artists have often portrayed those living in cities within advanced economies as feeling alone and sad in a crowd. Many people with plenty of material resources feel "poor" in the sense that no one cares about them. Finding a place where everyone is welcomed in a genuinely friendly fashion and then made to feel part of the established group can greatly upgrade the quality of life. Believers and nonbelievers alike should be attracted.

Lesson Six considers healing hurts and hang-ups. Regardless of a hurt's cause, it helps to talk with others who have had the same experience. In addition, understanding that God wants to heal the hurt with His love can be a great comfort and source of strength while dealing with difficult circumstances. Almost everyone has hang-ups, which are usually habitual reactions that serve no good purpose and might actually be causing harm. Becoming encouraged to eliminate such a hang-up could lead to greatly improving the quality of spiritual and daily life.

In Lesson Seven, we look into having more Kingdom experiences, occasions when His Kingdom is expanded or improved, in part, by what a believer has done. Such moments can be filled with joy and feeling God's closeness in wonderful ways. While people come to faith for a variety of reasons, it's unlikely that someone will do so primarily due to a desire to have Kingdom experiences. Such motivation is unlikely simply due to few nonbelievers ever hearing very much about the joys of walking with God and being in His will. When I teach discipleship courses, I'm often struck by how someone sharing an amazing experience with God can also cause some believers to reexamine the depth of their relationships with Jesus, simply due to having a greater appreciation of how wonderful drawing closer to Him can be.

We now begin with Lesson One: Correct Misunderstandings.

Lesson One:

Correct Misunderstandings

"I would have said, 'I will dash them in pieces,
I will make the memory of them to cease from among men,'
Had I not feared the wrath of the enemy,
Lest their adversaries should misunderstand,
Lest they should say, 'Our hand is high;
And it is not the LORD who has done all this.'"

— Deuteronomy 32:26-27 (NKJV)

In his final song before dying on Mount Nebo (Deuteronomy 32:26-27, NKJV), Moses related what God had told him about His attitude toward the Israelites. Due to God's anger at their disobedience, He would have totally erased the Hebrews from existence and memory had it not been for His concern that their nonbelieving enemies might misunderstand the consequences of His actions as being merely due to their own skills and strength. We should be similarly concerned that misunderstandings not cloud the minds of anyone, believer or nonbeliever, so that each one can draw closer to God and do more to expand and improve His Kingdom.

At the most surprising times, God sends me reminders of how much can be misunderstood about Him. I well remember an occasion when I had some repairs done to my car. While waiting to pay, a distraught woman began loudly declaring to the garage owner that she would never have a relationship with a god who allowed little children to suffer from painful, fatal diseases. Naturally, that wasn't the ideal moment or place to discuss her understanding of why suffering occurs. However, she clearly wasn't going to advance in developing any kind of relationship with God until she understood that God doesn't intend such things to happen, but, rather, that such afflictions occur in a broken world filled with sin resulting from human choices, sin that needs to be and can be totally redeemed by everyone repenting and following Jesus.

I often unintentionally overhear loud conversations while traveling during which someone will cite the Bible as "proof" that God is quite different from His actual nature. Most of such mischaracterizations appear to be well-meaning, often reflecting confusion caused by interpreting individual verses in isolation from the rest of the Bible. In other cases, misunderstandings of translations can cloud perceptions. For instance, some people don't realize that translations that speak about "fearing" God don't mean "fearing" in the sense of needing to worry about being harmed by a dangerous being, but that such "fearing" rather means humbling yourself as a sinner in a loving relationship with the all-powerful, positively focused, perfect God who only wants the best for you.

There's good news about such misunderstandings: Although virtually everyone begins by having the wrong impressions of God and His Kingdom, God is highly effective in using His Holy Spirit and the Bible to remedy any such mistaken views for new believers. In addition, many people decide to "check" what they think they understand about God for its accuracy. That checking may involve asking a pastor, doing a word search in an electronic version of the Bible, or praying for clarity. Rather than complain about God's nature with the next garage owner they meet, some may wish to go to an investigation center where people gladly and pleasantly help them assess their impressions, confusions, and misunderstandings.

So what kinds of misunderstandings might be occurring? As I mention in the introduction to Part One, few people can accurately describe God's nature, especially in terms of His allowing free will (so He can have meaningful relationships with each person). Even fewer can explain what God's Kingdom is (the community of believers and His presence within believers). Many others have become confused by observing Christians sinning, and incorrectly associating that behavior with how believers should behave.

God, His Kingdom, and the proper Christian behavior aren't the only things that most people misunderstand. I, for one, often make mistake after mistake in some activity that I cannot avoid doing but for which I have little skill. Here's a simple example. When something stops working at our house, I'm sometimes unsure what type of person I should hire to make repairs. The home originally drained the waste water from the kitchen sink and dishwasher into a cesspool in the front yard. When our backyard cesspool collapsed, an engineer told us that the town required it to be replaced with a septic system. Due to the stringent local ordinance in this regard, we had to build a system large enough for a small Holiday Inn. Those who put in the septic system told us that we didn't need to immediately connect the kitchen drain to it, "Just wait for the cesspool in front to collapse, then redirect the kitchen wastewater into the septic system and fill in the cesspool." Thirty-one years later, the front cesspool partially collapsed. While it was easy to find a plumber to redirect the kitchen waste water to the septic system, no one seemed to have a clue about what to do with the cesspool. Eventually, a handyman interpreted my direction to "fill it in" to mean putting gravel into rapidly widening surface holes leading down into the cesspool. While such a "fill in" kept people from falling into one of the holes, the ground above the cesspool would keep sinking until the collapse was complete. I was soon resigned to many years of adding layer after layer of gravel, sand, and dirt on top of the depression while it gradually deepened, until such time as the underlying cesspool was finally "filled up" from the top. Yet, presumably there was someone who would have first removed the top layers of soil, then done a great job filling in the collapsed cesspool, and been delighted to do the work. As you can imagine, I would be eager to overcome my misunderstandings about who to hire for what jobs. Perhaps other homeowners feel the same way.

The cesspool example shows that an investigation center might be able to help people answer a wide variety of misunderstandings, especially of the sort that almost everyone knows that they have. In addition, most people eventually realize that they "don't get" some other things about their lives. After receiving helpful assistance concerning one subject, someone might return for help with a different topic. What are some areas that people care about and often appreciate that they misunderstand? The list would change from time to time as the culture's focus shifts, but here are some often misunderstood topics that are likely to continue being of interest:

- Getting better grades in school while expending less time and effort
- Choosing a career that will provide the most satisfaction and flexibility
- Finding a spouse with whom to have a great marriage
- Developing a close, loving family
- Overcoming limited resources in providing for a family

- Helping children succeed
- Legally paying less in taxes
- Investing money more successfully
- Becoming healthier and more energetic
- Overcoming a personal crisis (such as the death of a loved one, divorce, serious illness, or financial reversal)

- Assisting elderly parents
- Improving quality of life
- Overcoming loneliness
- Developing a support network
- Preparing for retirement

Naturally, an investigation center can't begin to correct every misunderstanding, but dealing well with more than just ones related to knowing and understanding God should receive careful consideration. Here's another possibility: Provide a process at the investigation center for assessing what people might be misunderstanding, but don't yet appreciate that they misunderstand, in important areas of their lives. Such a process (potentially provided through a class or course) could direct people to resources that can provide proper understanding. Topics could be identified by a poll of what people who are located nearby believe about important topics. Where the beliefs are mistaken, the topic could be added to what the investigation center addresses.

I'm particularly intrigued by helping with mistaken beliefs because we may misunderstand even more things that we think we understand. The old observation, "It's as plain as the nose on your face," is only accurate if you are looking at someone else's face ... or your own face in a mirror. Otherwise, the last thing you are going to see is your nose. Some of such ignorance can be partly due to complacency. In other cases, fear of the unknown can discourage someone from looking into what they prefer to think they already understand.

Business people often display such shortsightedness. No matter how well paid or highly regarded the senior executives of a major company are, I usually find them to be unaware of how well or poorly their companies perform their most important activities as compared to the most effective organizations. Consequently, most executives will describe almost everything their companies do as being superior to other firms, while, in fact, it's rare for more than 4 percent of their activities to be conducted anywhere near what the most effective organizations accomplish.

Let me address another important source of misunderstandings: how we are perceived by others. Here's a personal example. As a youngster, I loved track and field. One of my events was sprinting, which requires a fast start followed by quick acceleration. I was pretty good and felt pleased about my skill. Then, one day my coach talked to me about learning the shot put. After encouraging me to switch, he commented, "You were built more for comfort than for speed." At the time, I didn't want to ask what he meant. Consequently, I puzzled over that observation for many years. My original perception was that he thought I was overweight, but I didn't think I was. Many years later, I happened to be standing next to a number of men my height in front of a large, long mirror. I noticed for the first time that my legs are much shorter in proportion to my torso than are the legs of other men my height. "So that's what the coach meant" was the thought that marked the end of my misunderstanding about how others saw me physically.

Naturally, if something so obvious can be misunderstood, imagine how much more likely it is that the nonphysical perceptions of others can also be misunderstood. Here's another personal example. As a management consultant, I have always enjoyed great success in persuading my clients to implement the recommendations I made. In my mind, the main reason for this effectiveness was the careful documentation I provided to clients about why the actions were the most useful ones. Imagine my surprise when an independent agent polled my clients about why they usually followed my recommendations: Clients reported that they were paying no attention to the documentation. In fact, many of them couldn't understand the supporting information. Instead, clients were paying close attention to how confident I seemed to be in my conclusions. When I appeared to have no doubts, they responded by acting. After understanding how these recommendations were being evaluated, I learned to better explain the documentation and more carefully monitored how well I was conveying my actual level of confidence in the conclusions.

In this regard, an investigation center could be a safe environment for people to learn more about how they are perceived by gaining candid comments from others. In the process, some people would be encouraged to change their attitudes and behaviors in ways that would benefit them and all those with whom they come into contact.

In the United States, immigration from a variety of countries has greatly increased. Consequently, there are many Americans who don't understand some of the newer cultures and are unwittingly making incorrect assumptions and acting inappropriately. Information centers could also be a God-sent resource for easing such misunderstandings and reducing their harmful effects. Immigrants might also find such centers to be helpful for gaining understanding of why their new culture acts in confusing ways.

While I could obviously write more about misunderstandings, I'm sure you more fully appreciate now the potential value of reducing them.

Lesson One Assignments

1. Where do you often see misunderstandings about God and His Kingdom?

2. How could investigation centers reduce such misunderstandings?

3. What other kinds of misunderstandings do you often notice?

4. How might investigation centers also help overcome these misunderstandings?

5. What personal misunderstandings could investigation centers help you eliminate?

Lesson Two:

Answer Questions

*Now when the queen of Sheba heard of the fame of Solomon
concerning the name of the LORD,
she came to test him with hard questions.*

— 1 Kings 10:1 (NKJV)

In Solomon's time, the queen of Sheba was one of the most powerful and richest rulers. While it was much more inconvenient and dangerous then to travel long distances, she was so attracted by the fame of Solomon's Godly wisdom that she made the difficult journey to Israel at great expense with a large entourage. Solomon's ability to answer hard questions convinced her of God's power and Solomon's connection to Him. If such a mighty and influential person had hard questions worth so much cost and effort to pose, this example suggests many other people may, as well. It's also highly likely that those who have been unsuccessful in pursuit of answers for some time will also put significant effort into their searches, even if they cannot afford to spend nearly as much in doing so as the queen of Sheba did. Such individuals may be prime candidates for information centers that can answer their most difficult and fundamental questions.

Receiving satisfying answers to important questions can also lead many of such people to return, as well as to draw first-time visitors who hear about such successful experiences. In addition, when God is given the credit for supplying the answers, interest in knowing more about God is sure to increase, as well, much as it did for the queen of Sheba.

Consider a secular parallel. In the early days of home-improvement retailer Home Depot, the company sponsored large numbers of do-it-yourself classes to help people more effectively fix or upgrade their homes. After gaining such knowledge, home owners bought more supplies at Home Depot. In the process, everyone benefited.

What are some important, unanswered questions that might attract people to an investigation center? As I mentioned in Part One's introduction, such questions might include: Why do bad things happen to "good" people? Where do people go after they die? Why should someone be baptized? What difference can attending church make? When will God answer my prayers? What is my calling?

Notice that people of different faiths will answer these questions in varying ways. Consequently, the most satisfying answers will be those that consider the evidence in light of all the answers someone is likely to hear. I'm sure you appreciate that providing such a satisfying answer is quite a bit harder than merely reciting what someone learned as a youngster in Sunday school or as an adult in a discipleship course.

Another challenge is that, unlike Solomon, no one at an investigation center may know anything about any aspect of the subject. I mention this possibility because my students often ask for my help with questions about which I have no knowledge. When such issues arise, I always offer to look for someone who knows the answer or to do the research myself. In doing so, I sometimes discover I've taken on more than I can accomplish and have to admit to defeat. On those occasions, I always apologize and explain my efforts to help. Students always seem to appreciate any sincere and careful attempts I have made, even when I fail to produce an answer. After experiencing many such reactions, I eventually grew more confident in encouraging people to seek answers from me. One step I took to do so was in choosing askdonmitchell@yahoo.com as one of my e-mail addresses. The most frequent reaction to giving someone that e-mail address is to be asked, "What can I ask you about?" I answer, "Anything." With the guidance of the Holy Spirit, I am able to assist everyone who asks a question at least a little, even if that is only by describing where and how the answer cannot be found.

Among those who have had no prior contact with an investigation center and who know nothing about the people who will be answering questions, only the individuals who are desperate for answers may willing to go there and ask. This limitation might be partially surmounted by having answerers demonstrate their expertise during well-attended outreach activities. While doing so, providing credibility for their answers will also be quite important. God through His Holy Spirit may choose to assist in supplying some confidence to hearers, as apparently occurred with the queen of Sheba. In the Biblical account of her meeting with Solomon, there's no evidence indicating that she independently tested the accuracy of what he answered before accepting the answers as true.

When an answer is counterintuitive, it may be essential to demonstrate the answer's accuracy in a way that few will dispute, especially if involving some activity that virtually everyone does ineffectively. Let's say the subject is making a good first impression. A demonstration could begin with a questioner privately posing his or her query about making a good first impression and also sharing her or his opinion of the right answer. If the questioner is wrong, the expert would then present a better answer. To demonstrate the answer's accuracy, the questioner might be given an immediate opportunity to try his or her approach with some strangers and then learn the strangers' reactions. New first impressions could next be gained by having the questioner apply the expert's approach with a different group of strangers and then hearing their initial impressions following the better approach.

Information centers could increase effectiveness by sharing with one another the questions that have been posed and the most helpful and impressive answers. In doing so, a more effective base of shared knowledge could be developed, possibly including audio and visual materials that could be provided to questioners at information centers. Such an approach could enable more people to experience impressive, prior demonstrations. Providing some of such evidence online could also help attract first-time visitors.

Some of the most pressing unanswered questions will undoubtedly relate to health issues. For instance, I was very persistent in seeking a way to eliminate the searing pain that I felt for 22 years in much of the left side of my body. During that time, I read, asked questions, and tried anything that anyone suggested might help. However, it was only after I asked two of my pastors to pray for me to be relieved of the pain that I gained blessed relief, relief that came in just a few minutes after a warm source of power slowly moved from the top of my body down to the bottom of my left foot ... permanently answering my question as well as satisfying my need. I would have greatly benefited from someone having suggested 22 years earlier that I ask for healing prayers of the sort described in the book of James ... but, alas, no one did. When God has been using a medical situation to gain someone's attention, receiving the answers to such questions will undoubtedly also lead the questioner to grow closer to Him as certainly happened in my case.

An investigation-center staff should always be in prayer about what questions to be able to answer, knowing that God will be sending people with those questions. Advance preparations can then be made for providing answers that will be more helpful and credible. In communities where local churches don't do much to educate believers in their faith, many questions about having a relationship with God can be anticipated. In such cases, it may be helpful to offer courses that address a large number of related questions, rather than just dealing with individual questions in isolation from one another about having a relationship with God.

I suspect that many of the people answering questions in information centers will have previously done so as experts in other contexts. By drawing on those prior experiences, it will be possible for answerers to anticipate many of the questions that will be posed in their areas of expertise and to draw on having helped others to do a better job of answering the center's questioners.

Naturally, a helpful answer may in some cases be to seek information elsewhere, in places where knowledge and information are effectively specialized in the topic, or helpful equipment and necessary resources are available. In making this comment, I'm reminded of the way that some of the world's famous medical diagnostic centers (such as the Mayo Clinic) play a valuable role in pinning down the causes of mysterious health problems. After an accurate diagnosis is made, patients are usually referred for ongoing treatments to excellent medical centers located near the patients' homes. An information center will often be helpful in a similar way.

While there are an infinite number of unanswered questions, only God knows all of the answers. However, answering some unanswered questions is a powerful way to draw eager knowledge seekers to information centers. While there, the answers that are received will often stimulate still more questions ... until the questioner gains a fuller sense of the kind of life that God intends for him or her.

Lesson Two Assignments

1. What questions do you hear others asking about God and His Kingdom?

2. How could investigation centers helpfully answer such questions?

3. What other kinds of questions do you hear people eagerly seeking answers to?

4. How might investigation centers also help with answering these questions?

5. What are the most pressing questions that you would like to have answered?

Lesson Three:

Satisfy Curiosity

Now an angel of the Lord spoke to Philip, saying,
"Arise and go toward the south along the road
which goes down from Jerusalem to Gaza." This is desert.

So he arose and went. And behold, a man of Ethiopia,
a eunuch of great authority
under Candace the queen of the Ethiopians,
who had charge of all her treasury,
and had come to Jerusalem to worship, was returning.

And sitting in his chariot, he was reading Isaiah the prophet.

Then the Spirit said to Philip, "Go near and overtake this chariot."

So Philip ran to him, and heard him reading the prophet Isaiah,
and said, "Do you understand what you are reading?"

And he said, "How can I, unless someone guides me?"

And he asked Philip to come up and sit with him.

— Acts 8:26-31 (NKJV)

Despite curiosity seldom being as strong and as long-lasting a motivation as a desire for an answer to an important question with significant consequences, curiosity can paradoxically often lead to taking action ahead of all other motivations. If you doubt that observation, just remember the last time you went on the Internet to perform a given task and ended up being distracted by something else you accidentally found there. If you are like me, in the process of satisfying your curiosity about the unexpected information you may have even forgotten what brought you to the Internet and shut down the computer without having accomplished your original purpose.

In these verses from Acts 8:26-31 (NKJV), we see such an example of curiosity in action. The eunuch appears to have been the ancient-world equivalent of the chief financial officer for a major ruler, Candace, queen of the Ethiopians. While his normal work undoubtedly related to financial planning, levying taxes, protecting the proceeds, authorizing and checking expenditures, and ensuring that the queen was not cheated, the eunuch had somehow acquired a scroll that contained the prophetic book of Isaiah. Much like an Internet surfer, this man was trying to make sense of something intriguing he had found, even though he knew that understanding it without help was impossible. Because the Holy Spirit was at work, Philip was directed to meet the eunuch and he explained Isaiah's words about the Messiah. Before not much more time passed that day, the eunuch became a believer in Jesus and was baptized. Church tradition credits this encounter with having helped to launch the Christian faith in Ethiopia. Whether or not that tradition is accurate, certainly the eunuch was able to satisfy his curiosity about God and Salvation and to become a believer, a result that must have caused angels to cheer in heaven.

In my late teens and early twenties, it was common for people my age to investigate a wide variety of faiths. In most cases, people I knew did so due to wanting to follow a faith that they had deliberately chosen, rather than simply following the faith they knew from their childhoods. At the time, I was extremely surprised by how many choices there were, many of which were completely new to me. One of the great benefits of satisfying my curiosity about other faiths was to confirm and strengthen my faith in Jesus, His Father, and the Holy Spirit. While engaging in this investigation, however, I was disappointed to find that I could not locate objective comparisons of the various faiths. Instead, I had to draw my own conclusions after reading some texts of different major religions during college courses and in personal studies.

However, reaching such a conclusion about strengthening faith in and a relationship with God should not be assumed. I met many people then and later who were so attracted by new non-Christian faiths they learned about while young that they were still following such beliefs many decades later. After asking about their decisions, I have usually found that they had deeply studied the faith that was new to them, often without making a similar investigation of their prior or other faiths. For instance, I know a highly regarded Jewish man who found the Buddhist focus on losing connection to the material world so appealing that he has been happily practicing and evangelizing Buddhism ever since. I get the sense that he found just moving beyond a focus on materialism to be quite satisfying, never realizing that Jesus could provide much more. Hopefully, this Buddhist's example will make us more aware that some people may be satisfied by finding a "better" faith than what they know about the faith they know best (regardless of how little they know about it), rather than carefully checking out the major choices. An investigation center will need to be prepared to help such faith comparison shoppers do their homework well.

While searches to find a satisfying faith are more common among younger people, I suspect that such searches also occur relatively frequently among people at older ages who have just experienced major life challenges (such as the death of a loved one, divorce, long-term unemployment, bankruptcy, serious accident, chronic illness, addiction, victimization, or disability). An investigation center should be prepared to receive people who will be seeking to satisfy their curiosity about what to do in light of their recent, painful experiences and any resulting, difficult circumstances. In such contexts, it will often be most valuable for these seekers to engage with others who have had the same experiences and who also looked for answers to why these circumstances happened to them, as well as for answers about what to do next. In doing so, someone with such curiosity will often benefit from meeting with several similarly experienced people of different ages and backgrounds, as well as those who have been removed from such events for longer as well as shorter lengths of time, in order to gain more and better perspectives on such occurrences.

A third group that investigation centers should consider helping is teenagers still living at home. The desire is strong among most teenagers to create a separate identify from the one provided by their family and initial station in life. In seeking such an identity, either being "cool" or somehow obtaining greater popularity can be viewed as quite important. Those who find it difficult to accomplish either objective may feel as if their lives don't have much purpose and meaning. For all such individuals, an information center could be a haven where a wider perspective on life and choices could help them to explore and find ideas and beliefs that will better serve them. While young people usually act as if they are immortal, many of them actually accept the reality of their mortality and find questions about what happens after death to be painful. If a family doesn't provide good role models, it's also easy for such young people to fall into a general state of rebellion that will simply make it harder for them to determine and act on their life's purposes and callings. In many cases, teens will benefit from gaining mentors who will stay involved until the teens are more firmly established in Godly life directions. Of course, if those who find it easy to be cool or popular would also like to know more about what other kinds of identity are possible, God can provide them with something better, as well.

I don't want to leave this lesson without mentioning two other groups that might be served: the aged and the idle. In many nations, people are living longer than ever. However, due to the geographic dispersion of their families, more frequent divorce, and more difficulties in finding work near their original homes, people can enter their so-called Golden Years with few people living nearby who know them well. Come up against any of the predictable life challenges of older age (such as living on a fixed income, needing to find better health care, getting around when that's physically difficult, forgetting more, and declining hearing and vision) without access to people who can help, and life can seem like something better discarded than embraced for its full potential. An investigation center might have to engage in outreach (including, but not limited to, visiting people in their homes, providing transportation to and from the investigation center, bringing information to people, and helping with certain activities) to serve such individuals well.

I mention the aged and the idle at the same time because the two groups may include some of the same individuals. People are being let go from their jobs at younger and younger ages, and there may not be very many paying jobs they can physically handle during the last third of their lives. In addition, since the global economic difficulties during the first decade of the twenty-first century, many young people have found it hard to establish careers and families. Such people can easily be drawn into pursuits that pull them away from God, as well as from expanding and improving His Kingdom. An investigation center can be a wonderful way for such individuals to find what God has planned for them to do and to feel the love and peace of engaging in these activities.

Someone who has plenty of time to spend on satisfying curiosity can potentially develop a strong interest in whatever is uncovered. When that happens, other benefits can accrue, including developing friends with similar interests, identifying enjoyable activities, and finding valuable new perspectives concerning other aspects of life. When such connections occur, some of those who have developed such a passion will become interested in sharing what they have learned with others. Ultimately some of the people providing answers at an investigation center may well have first entered one seeking to satisfy some curiosity of their own.

Once again, I think there is a benefit from polling those who live and work nearby to find out what they are curious about, especially in terms of interests that have not been satisfied by Internet searches and other readily available resources. In doing so, programs concerning such interests should be a strong draw for attracting the first visitors to an investigation center.

Such a draw will be increased where "hands-on" experience is essential to gaining full knowledge and skill. Rather than relying on providing "expert" answers and discussions, I suspect that investigation centers will do their best work by providing experiences. God often uses curiosity to draw someone toward one of His purposes. However, many people will be reluctant to participate in the ways that He intends until they have had an appealing experience. For instance, suburbanites usually have some trepidation about serving in urban homeless shelters. Yet, everyone I have brought to do such work ended up feeling quite happy to have had the experience. In fact, just the other day I assisted a high school student who was answering a question on a college application about what activities she would never give up. She responded by describing her permanent commitment to serving at a homeless shelter, due to the inspiration she gained from seeing the women residents patiently and gracefully deal with their difficulties.

Since almost anything can stir curiosity, especially when God intends to attract attention in a given way, helping people who are curious can be a powerful way to serve Him and to expand and improve God's Kingdom. I also suspect that helping others make such connections will be especially rewarding for those who do so. Perhaps you are one of the people God has called to serve in one of these ways. What joy awaits you!

Lesson Three Assignments

1. What is it about God and His Kingdom that draws the greatest curiosity among people you know?

2. How could investigation centers helpfully satisfy such curiosity?

3. What other kinds of unsatisfied curiosity do many people have?

4. How might investigation centers also help with information and experiences about these interests?

5. About what do you have unsatisfied curiosity?

Lesson Four:

Overcome Discomfort

What fruit did you have then
in the things of which you are now ashamed?
For the end of those things is death.

— Romans 6:21 (NKJV)

Do you know what it feels like to have a queasy feeling in the pit of your stomach after having made a serious error, one that you deeply regret and expect to cause many painful future problems? Such a reaction is familiar to most people. They began experiencing it while quite young, after doing something that they knew was wrong for which there would be undesirable consequences, whether being yelled at, punished, or shamed in front of others.

As Romans 6:21 (NKJV) suggests, the action that ultimately led to feeling the discomfort might have initially appeared to promise some benefit that was hard to resist at the time. Prior to acting, seldom will the thought have entered the person's mind of having ongoing discomfort after taking the action. Unfortunately, the discomfort will later prove to be much greater and longer lasting than any sought benefit.

If you need a specific example of what this can be like, I'm reminded of a man who was always quick to criticize married men who committed adultery. He would bring up the subject every time I was with him, even when there was no apparent reason for doing

27

so. Later, his wife discovered that this same man had been doing what he criticized others for, and she divorced him. When he and I had lunch a few years afterward, his face and voice were filled with pain for having caused the break-up of his family. This time he did not bring up the subject of married men committing adultery.

For those who aren't yet in a relationship with Jesus, such feelings of discomfort (whether experienced as shame, regret, self-pity, or something else) are all too familiar. Why? The individual often feels that he or she has no way to relieve the burden that is so strongly and painfully felt. Thus, long-ago mistakes can continue to cause daily pain. Each subsequent error piles on still more unrelieved pain, making the overall burden harder and harder to bear.

Here's another example. A man had long been an alcoholic. Because of this self-abuse, he often made errors in judgment, especially by foolishly spending money he needed for important matters. During those years, his wife had entrusted him with her retirement savings. Without telling her, the man spent every penny of the savings. Just before dying, he began to hint that she would be broke after he was gone. She didn't take the hint, and he apparently never confessed to her what he had done. Naturally, the sad discovery hit her quite hard at a vulnerable time. Yet, I suspect that his unrelieved guilt over having taken and spent her money probably caused him even more pain than she experienced due to his betrayal and her unexpectedly reduced retirement circumstances. I don't know if he ever confessed and repented this sin to God. If he didn't, life must have seemed like a terrible burden while carrying such guilt. While only God knows if he sought His forgiveness for his sins, I certainly hope that he did so.

While this second example is an extreme one, many people carry deep, ongoing pain over actions (or failures to act) that took place long ago. Let me share yet another example to help you appreciate this point. A woman I knew enjoyed dining out and having a few drinks. On such occasions, her husband would usually be more cautious in his alcohol consumption and drive them home. However, one night she drove while intoxicated. While I don't know the details of what happened, I later learned that there was a traffic accident during which someone in another car was killed. The immediate consequences were severe for the woman: She was arrested and tried for manslaughter. She pled guilty. Because there was a mandatory sentence of one year, she served that term in prison ... something she found to be very difficult. The longer-term results were also severe. After the prison term was over, she wasn't allowed to drive for many years, undoubtedly reminding her of what she had done wrong. Guilt feelings must also have been strong. I'm sure this woman would have done almost anything to have been able to go back, not have those drinks, and not have contributed to someone's death. Yet, there is no undoing such a result. Only through the sacrifice of our Lord, Jesus Christ, faith in Him, and repentance can forgiveness be received that will bring peace. I hope she eventually found peace in this way. While few people have caused someone else's death, almost everyone has caused emotional pain that led to ongoing regret until forgiveness was received. I hope all of them will also receive the peace that Jesus desires to provide.

If you think about these three examples, I'm sure you'll agree that the people involved were probably not looking for opportunities to share their stories in public with strangers. Yet, there must have been times when they wondered how they could better deal with the consequences of what they had done. Would any of them have come to an investigation center? Only God knows, but clearly the reputation of an investigation center for alleviating discomfort would have had to have been very great before any of them would have been attracted, actually gone there, and then spoken up. In addition, the investigation center would have had to have avoided giving the impression that people coming there would be judged in any way ... or put into any unwanted situations.

Investigation centers will probably not be recruiting their attendees nightly from among those who are falling down drunk at local taverns, just been served with divorce papers, or indicted for serious crimes. However, thinking about such individuals reminds us of the desirability of lessening such discomfort for those suffering it without their having to publicly reveal any embarrassing details. A possible approach for investigation centers could be to offer classes about finding peace for anyone who feels weighed down by life's burdens, without specifying what those burdens might be except to describe them in nonthreatening, kind ways.

I suspect these classes might work well based on my experiences with teaching adult discipleship classes. While no one who attends such classes is required or asked to share any personal information, many people do. Some of the burdens that they have carried due to past actions would crush a dump truck. After beginning to gain peace during the classes, such individuals seem to then substantially increase their peacefulness by describing what they have done or experienced, and then seeing that others react sympathetically. Thus, for many of those who are so burdened, sharing what they are feeling becomes a valuable part of the healing process.

Having started off by discussing very substantial sources of discomfort, it's easy to lose sight of the many minor kinds of discomfort that people would also like to shed or reduce. In many cultures, for instance, attractiveness, youth, and being slim are highly praised, leaving many of those who have none of these characteristics feeling dissatisfied with themselves and their lives. The number of people engaging in cosmetic surgery, using powerful cosmetics, and dieting is always increasing. Having been on many diets myself, I can certainly sympathize with those who feel less than satisfied with their appearance. It took me a long time to realize that God cares about my heart for Him and other people, as well as my health (so I can serve Him and His Kingdom as part of an abundant life), rather than about my appearance. Gaining such insight has greatly changed how I focus my time and attention. Undoubtedly, because anyone can make at least some improvements in becoming closer to God and others and living healthier lives, many people would be pleased to learn God's perspective concerning what we should emphasize.

Here's another common source of discomfort: I often meet believers who would like to marry and have a family, but who have not yet been able to find a suitable person, despite much attending of church singles' groups, various kinds of dating, and Godly volunteering. In private, these individuals often describe feeling quite sad about the lack of such a relationship. In some cases, God may have a person in mind for eventual marriage, but the time isn't yet right. In other cases, God may not intend for an individual to marry. I don't know which Godly intention applies to which person, and neither do the people who wonder. Until God's will is either accomplished or made clear concerning a spouse, I suspect that courses and testimonies that address how deepening a relationship with God can be remarkably fulfilling might be of some benefit for reducing the discomfort of such believers.

Despite being attractive, vibrant, and slim, a young person can have other painful sources of discomfort. While teaching high school students ways to improve grades, score higher on college entrance exams, and be more appealing to college admission officers, I learn about unbelievably embarrassing personal problems that some teens have experienced, ones that they feel acutely long after the problems have been overcome ... due to peers and their parents remembering the youngster's prior difficulties. For instance, some young people have speech quirks that may make it hard to understand them, cause them to sound "babyish," or even to give some people the impression that they are mentally disturbed. I suspect that many of such youngsters live in fear of their problems returning or of someone embarrassing them with reminders of past difficulties.

Other youngsters may simply feel awkward because they cannot afford the stylish clothes that the wealthiest students wear. I remember working for my father's lawn service business as a teen, cutting grass and weeding in the neighborhoods where many of my more affluent friends lived. I would see them heading off looking stylish to play golf at the country club while I was covered in dust, grime, and sweat in a filthy t-shirt and shorts.

In both kinds of circumstances, there's a blessing when such a youngster can learn genuine humility, an appreciation for receiving kind words from someone who doesn't have to be kind, and understanding that true goodness isn't indicated by what you look like or how you sound. While I now greatly appreciate God's thoughtfulness in providing me with such humbling experiences, no one helped me to see the benefits at the time. Certainly, many youngsters who are receiving such Godly lessons would probably appreciate gaining these insights while they are feeling confused about burdens they have that others don't.

Another common source of discomfort relates to family difficulties. It's more common than not for siblings to avoid one another, rather than to enjoy one another's company, after their parents no longer provide a pleasant context for a family connection. In fact, when the second parent dies, there's often squabbling over estates and possessions that can leave one and all feeling emotionally hurt and materially injured. In some cases, divorce and remarriage can leave a parent or a child embittered. One man had a very difficult marriage that ended in a divorce while his only child, a daughter, was quite young. His ex-wife later told the young woman that the man often abused the daughter in some very nasty ways while she was a baby. Naturally, the daughter wanted nothing to do with her father, but he would have liked nothing better than to see her occasionally. While I don't know the facts of the situation (only God does), I suspect that an investigation center could do a real service by counseling those who would like to repair family relationships that have been tattered by wrongs, whether real or falsely attributed.

Since God is love and wants us to love Him and one another, His love can so infuse the activities of an investigation center that more people can feel and be healed by that love. What could be better? Clearly, an investigation center has to avoid any of the reputational baggage that keeps some people from drawing closer to God, such as assuming that "holier than thou" believers will go out of their way to make a person filled with discomfort feel even worse, or that those who feel discomfort will be pointed out as public examples to be shunned. We must always keep Jesus' love in mind, helping us to delight in the person who wants to be closer to Him and is developing a repentant heart, regardless of what that person has done in the past.

Lesson Four Assignments

1. What are the greatest causes of discomfort among people you know?

2. How could investigation centers helpfully reduce or eliminate such discomfort?

3. What other kinds of unrelieved discomfort do many people have?

4. How might investigation centers also help to relieve these sorts of discomfort?

5. What causes you discomfort that you would like to reduce or eliminate?

6. What could make an investigation center seem more attractive and welcoming to those who need relief from their discomfort?

Lesson Five:

Find Friendly Fellowship

This is the message which we have heard from Him and declare to you,
that God is light and in Him is no darkness at all.
If we say that we have fellowship with Him,
and walk in darkness, we lie and do not practice the truth.
But if we walk in the light as He is in the light,
we have fellowship with one another,
and the blood of Jesus Christ His Son cleanses us from all sin.

— 1 John 1:5-7 (NKJV)

Few people desire to live as hermits; most of us are seeking friendly fellowship with others. While first meeting new people, everyone is usually on her or his best behavior, and conversations usually go well. Later, difficulties arise often enough with the new connections that most people are soon out looking for a newer source of friendly fellowship. As 1 John 1:5-7 (NKJV) tells us, all believers should be walking in the light simply due to being in fellowship with Jesus. If believers aren't behaving in that way, they are not practicing God's truth. Assuming an investigation center is careful to recruit people who are in deep and abiding relationships with Jesus and who seek to have the same kind of relationships with others, friendly fellowship should be more often the norm at the centers than will occur at most other places.

Think about the people you know. How many of them are over-ly busy due to having too much friendly fellowship with Godly peo-ple? I suspect that the list is quite short, if there are any names on it at all. Why? The friendly fellowship that God intends for us to have is filled with love, consideration, kindness, and caring. Having such fellowship provides other benefits, such as by strengthening and en-couraging us to do more of whatever else He requires. While it's common for someone to feel a lack of enough friendly fellowship with others, too much of such fellowship would seem to be impos-sible. The experience would, instead, probably feel more like having an unexpected extra week of paid vacation.

Feeling a lack of friendly fellowship is almost always based (at least in part) in failing to have enough of a relationship with Jesus. Yet, few people (including many believers) realize, and even fewer act on, that lesson. While it would be nice for people to quickly appreciate that they will never have a human relationship as good as the one they can have with Jesus, grasping that wonderful op-portunity typically begins only after first developing friendly fel-lowship with someone already in a strong and abiding relationship with Jesus.

There's a lesson in these observations for choosing who plays what roles at investigation centers. God wisely gifts each person dif-ferently for serving Him. Consequently, those who are attracting volunteers for investigation centers should look for people whom God has generously gifted to make anyone feel welcome under almost any circumstances. The most gifted of such individuals are better choices for greeting people when they arrive and for answering ques-tions about the investigation center and its activities.

While some people can very naturally play any aspect of such a welcoming or informational role, I have lately been impressed by meeting people who have been called to play such a role, but who didn't initially have much natural skill for doing so. In such cases, believers became effective in these roles after asking God to guide them to take the right actions and to say the most loving things. Following such supernatural guidance, these individuals gradually became more adept at making other people feel welcome in ways that eventually seemed quite natural to everyone else.

Because of such potential for learning to make people feel welcome, an investigation center should also be sure to teach welcoming ways to all those who will be serving there. Such training should emphasize the heart connection that Jesus wants us to have in loving others, emulating how He loves us no matter what we do or who we are.

While we are all familiar with how business employees are often trained to say certain things to customers when they arrive or leave, we all know that such training is ineffective in influencing us to return unless the words are drawn from genuine interest and concern. Otherwise, rote recitation in a monotone with averted eyes can become a source of annoyance ... and actually feel like unfriendliness.

For example, Starbucks tries to present a friendly image by having cashiers ask customers for their names so that the names can be repeated with a smile by the staff members who prepare and deliver the beverages. While that approach is better than not being asked for your name, the procedure can actually seem pretty hollow when it's just "lip service." For instance, I have been going to the same Starbucks at least 30 times a year for over a decade, yet I am asked for my name by the cashier almost every time ... even though my name is clearly printed on the Starbucks card I have just handed to the cashier for payment. I feel silly when that occurs.

Following Starbucks' company procedure can also have an unintended humorous side when one of the baristas there has the same first name as I do. When "Don" is on duty, the cashier will almost always make a point of introducing us to each other. Each "introduction" (of which I've had dozens with "Don") is as if it's for the first time, making the experience comical for me, as the cashier does her or his best to be friendly. However, "Don" looks at me each time with surprise, much the way I would peer at a total stranger I had unexpectedly bumped into while stepping backwards. I wonder if barista "Don" will ever remember having met me before. Starbucks would do better to, instead, tell me a new joke each time I pay. Such an approach would feel much more like having friendly fellowship with the staff.

While attracting people to enter and engage in activities at an investigation center can be extremely valuable for expanding and improving God's Kingdom, it will be hard to succeed in doing so unless there is a very strong preexisting appeal. How might such appeal be developed? One possible method is by offering events that will be popular and inevitably involve interactions with several people who share some mutual interest. Here's an example. Most poets love to read their work aloud to knowledgeable listeners who share their reactions to the poems. If having such an opportunity to gain reactions requires previously attending several such events as a commenting listener, many poets would be happy to play these roles, too.

Because almost everyone differs in what will bring him or her to attend an activity or event for the first time, an investigation center will undoubtedly need to program a large variety of choices before significantly increasing its destination appeal. Again, surveys of people who live and work in the local area can help an investigation center to develop an initial list of what activities, courses, and programs to offer. Knowing what events could draw people will also help in choosing more effective volunteers.

I also believe that the most appealing types of activities and events will shift quite a lot over time, depending on what's topical. Immediately after watching with others at the center a televised debate by presidential candidates just before an election, a discussion of the debate might be attractive to some. In a year when the economy is weak and jobs are scarce, job-seeking workshops might be quite the draw to people looking for work. During fashion week in New York, young people who want to dress in the latest styles might meet to discuss their reactions to what is being shown on runways before the ready-to-wear versions appear on retailers' shelves.

Naturally, finding friendly fellowship with other attendees, rather than just with the volunteers and staffers, will be one of the most effective approaches for attracting people to an investigation center. For me, working together for a number of times on a project has most often created a lasting bond with new people. In the course of doing something with others, I learn to respect and become more interested in them, even if all we do is be a team during a brief sports competition. With a name like "investigation center," it would be natural for some of the activities and events available at the center to enable trying new things, while being aided by people who are quite skilled at explaining and in demonstrating what to do. If there were no charge for the initial session, many people would be tempted to try, especially for any activities that most people describe as "fun" or "satisfying." As an example, I remember when a consulting client firm made flight simulators available for other clients at an event. While many of the attending executives were pilots, none of them had flown a large commercial jet. Through the simulators, the pilots were able to have as close to such experience as one could without actually flying such an aircraft. If we had also offered simulations of flying jet fighters during combat, I'm sure the appeal would have been even greater among the aggressive male executives who mostly comprised our clientele.

From the perspective of an investigation center, the best experiences for trying something new should include substantial engagement with people who aren't staff members or volunteers. I saw this kind of engagement done quite well during a seminar held by a well-known consulting firm. The event included an opportunity to improve output and quality in a simulated factory. The ideas generated were then applied at the various "work stations." After each ten-minute "work shift," everyone shared the next set of ideas based on the experiences. The group quickly gelled into one where respect for and interest in one another grew based on their contributions. For instance, while a prominent billionaire CEO was one participant, he received no more attention from anyone than the quality of his suggestions deserved.

Learning about anything could, of course, be organized to occur in groups. While doing so might at first seem like merely trying to throw people together, I think there's a more substantial reason for doing so.

Let me explain by sharing an example. I'm reminded of a man who is a legend in the teaching field. His math students, despite coming from economically poor families in an underdeveloped country, routinely outperform privileged students who attend the most elite schools in the world. While he applies many different methods to accomplish this enviable result, he strongly credits an important part of his success to having students of all skill levels work together in groups to "teach" one another how to solve math problems.

My own experience echoes the wisdom of this method. While in high school, I often studied math with a friend who found the material to be harder to grasp than I did. Most afternoons after school, I explained how to do the problems. In the course of doing so, she would eventually pick up what she didn't understand in class. I also found that having to "spell out" what was involved required me to transform my fairly intuitive appreciation into a logical explanation that made sense to my friend. Developing such explanations deepened my understanding. In addition, if I misunderstood something but didn't realize it, she would "pin" me with a question that made me realize I needed to take a fresh look. As a result, I feel that we both learned math from working together. In turn, she would often kindly explain things to me that I didn't understand about how others looked at what was going on at school. Her social intelligence was, thus, a good complement to my mathematical one. We both enjoyed high school much more as a result, and due to the bond we built during those afternoons our friendship continued after those study times.

As you can see from this last example, friendly fellowship increases when there is reciprocity of learning. Hopefully, the person who comes to an investigation center to gain a sense of how to do something will eventually be showing others how to do still other things, drawing on having had a good learning experience to then help others in an even friendlier, more helpful, and kinder way.

Many people just like to have a place to hang out where they can bump into people they know or would like to meet. I'm struck by how often people have reached out to me in a friendly way simply because they have often seen me in some place that I frequent. As a result, I've developed many friendly relationships with people who share common interests.

I think this tendency and preference for meeting in public is increased by the reluctance many people have today to invite others to their homes, reflecting often-justified concerns about becoming vulnerable or putting too much effort into what is merely an exploratory contact. For those who have such concerns, I believe that investigation centers can be an exceptionally good place to hang out, especially if a center is large enough to permit people to be there in both structured and unstructured ways without disturbing one another.

As a teenager, coffee houses that featured performances by unpaid, local folk singers played that role for me and many of my friends. These outlets were located close to nearby colleges and attracted a crowd of people too young to go to a bar. Since most people there were college students, it seemed awfully sophisticated and interesting for me as a high school student to listen to the music while sipping coffee. The music wasn't nonstop, so there was plenty of time to talk about whatever was on my mind with my friends, topics we would not have discussed at any of our homes, where our parents or siblings might have overheard what interested or concerned us. Perhaps investigation centers could play a similar role for some of today's teenagers.

I'm sure that there are many other ways to make investigation centers operate as places where friendly fellowship will begin and flourish. We'll explore some more of these ways in future lessons.

Lesson Five Assignments

1. What do people you know want to gain from having more friendly fellowship?

2. How could investigation centers help people gain more of such fellowship?

3. What other reasons cause people to look for friendly fellowship?

4. How else might investigation centers help people find satisfying forms of such fellowship?

5. What kinds of friendly fellowship would you like to increase in your life?

6. What could make an investigation center seem more appealing to those who want more friendly fellowship?

Lesson Six:

Heal Hurts and Hang-Ups

But God composed the body, having given greater honor
to that part which lacks it,
that there should be no schism in the body,
but that the members should have the same care for one another.
And if one member suffers, all the members suffer with it;
or if one member is honored, all the members rejoice with it.

— 1 Corinthians 12:24-26 (NKJV)

In 1 Corinthians 12:24-26 (NKJV), the Apostle Paul described the implications of having a diversity of spiritual gifts in the Body of Christ, designed by God to be unified in ways that will best expand and improve God's Kingdom. The image presented is the opposite of what we see hurt animals do. A wounded creature often withdraws to some quiet, undisturbed place to nurse its injuries, even if they are mortal ones. Humans often act in a similar way, slinking off to a place where they can be miserable alone to deal with their emotional hurts and unrelieved physical pain. However, Paul presented a different picture, one in which each believer is diminished by anyone who suffers. John Donne's well-known poem, "No Man Is an Island," expresses the same notion. The foundation for this connection, of course, comes from God's love for us, a love that cannot be diminished by what we do or don't do, believe or don't believe.

One way to show God's love is by having investigation centers help relieve hurts and reduce hang-ups. By "hurts" I mean anything that causes someone to feel pain, or significant physical or emotional discomfort. By "hang-ups" I mean patterns of thought that trigger behaviors that don't serve (and may even harm) God's Kingdom and God's plan for that individual.

You might be wondering why I cover "hurts" and "hang-ups" together in this lesson. Well, in most cases, hang-ups are responses to past hurts that people incorrectly believe will help them to avoid future pain or danger. As a result, to fully help someone who has been hurt, we will often need to assist in erasing any related hang-ups that linger after the hurt has been alleviated.

While most physical hurts are more than an investigation center should attempt to treat, I believe that the option of seeking healing through prayer should be made available to any such sufferers. Otherwise, many believers who could be supernaturally healed by God may not cleanse their hearts and then seek relief in faith through righteous prayers. Whether such prayers occur at an investigation center doesn't matter, just as long as sincere prayers are made in unquestioning faith.

Emotional hurts are more typical of the harm that can be helpfully addressed by investigation centers. Possible sources of healing can be based in faith, spending time with others who have experienced the same kinds of hurts, and talking about how to respond to and overcome the hurts. While it will be tempting for an investigation center to take on helping with any kind of emotional hurt, effectiveness will be poor in some instances unless specialization has occurred. For instance, if no one at the investigation center has experienced a certain kind of hurt, the visitor seeking help may not feel God's love as fully as would occur when assisted by someone with such experience. In communities that have a number of nearby investigation centers, it may be helpful to refer people to centers where those who have suffered certain kinds of less common hurts are willing and able to help those freshly experiencing such pain.

While it's obvious that people who have been hurt should be given loving support, investigation centers should also provide assistance designed to reduce the effects of common emotional hurts before they are experienced. For instance, almost everyone knows the pain of having lost a valued relationship. Having learned some of the better ways to deal with such experiences before they occur can make the resulting pain fade faster, hopefully by people increasing reliance on a relationship with Jesus rather than on being with the people they once dated. While no one might sign up for a course describing "How to Be Prepared When Someone Dumps You," the topic could naturally be addressed as a small part of a course for those who want to meet more people and have better dating experiences. Similarly, dealing with a parent's death could be a sliver of a course on how to help aging parents with their physical and psychological problems. In the same way, how to handle long-term unemployment could be a section of a course about how to have a more vibrant career. I mention these possibilities because in the same way that inoculating someone with polio vaccine reduces the likelihood and extent of having any later physical pain and dysfunction, preparing someone for likely emotional hurts can create somewhat similar benefits for reducing the degree and duration of harm.

While it's obviously helpful to prepare people for being emotionally hurt, it can be even more useful to assist those who have been hurt in avoiding any resulting hang-ups. In this regard, courses can again be a good idea. A common hang-up is avoiding situations that appear to be similar to the ones that caused hurts. Let me explain what I mean through an example. Let's imagine a young woman who has had bad experiences with the men she has dated. Because she is quite capable and emotionally strong, she first attracted a man who was perfectly happy letting her call all the shots and simply mimicking her activities and interests. She found this relationship unsatisfying in the extreme. As a result, she developed a hang-up about avoiding men who are flexible. Naturally, doing so led her into a relationship with a man who wanted to dictate her every word and deed. Of course, being with that man was more like slavery than being in a loving relationship. After deciding he wasn't for her, she had trouble keeping this man at a distance. Her next approach was to seek men who thought the same way as she did. She didn't realize that approach was going to be boring because the other person wouldn't bring much to the relationship. These experiences demonstrated a hang-up that would continue to cause her difficulties. By always heading in a quite different direction from what she last did in relationships, she would just end up engaging in another extreme relationship that would eventually prove to be unsatisfying for a new reason. If she had, instead, first learned what to look for in a relationship, she could have avoided many hurts and the difficulties that her hang-up caused. However, it's never too late. Whenever she refocuses on learning the right lessons about seeking relationships in the context of God's love, her hurts would gradually ebb and getting rid of her hang-up would mean not incurring as many new hurts.

Offering such prevention courses can provide another potential benefit: People who have attended such a course will have had an opportunity to appreciate the investigation center as a place to come for support after such hurts have occurred. Further, some of those who have taken a course and later been supported can eventually become volunteers who teach and support others, making the investigation center's help more effective. In addition, those who take on such roles will find themselves benefiting in unexpected ways that will improve their personal recoveries from hurts.

Keep in mind that many people don't realize when they have hang-ups. In fact, the more compulsive someone is while exercising such hang-ups, the less likely the person is to notice the hang-up. Why? Well, engaging in the compulsive behavior often relaxes people a bit, making less apparent the source of what causes them to feel uncomfortable.

I was reminded of this aspect of compulsive behavior by a student preparing for a graduate-school entrance examination. By the time we met, this man had taken every possible test-preparation course, as well as answered almost every question available from prior official tests and test-preparation companies. He was initially pleased when I assigned him to do a lot of testing in a short period of time. During the first lesson after doing such testing, I observed him engaging in several practices that were sure to cause problems, such as rereading every part of the test material from four to six times. While he felt that this "careful" reading approach would cause him to never make mistakes, he actually made more mistakes by overly filling his mind with information irrelevant to answering the questions and by taking so long that he couldn't answer all of the questions in the allotted time.

To improve, I suggested a more selective focus on the passages and concentrating any rereading solely on material related to answering the questions. I could immediately tell that he was dissatisfied with this suggestion: This approach did not fit with his hang-up, his compulsion to make a thorough, maximum effort. He kept referring to my proposed way of reading the material as "superficial." Of course, he shouldn't do any superficial reading during the test: He should be doing careful, "selective" reading that concentrates on the material that would improve his score.

Certainly, if he hadn't been a slow reader, he could have exercised his compulsion and still been quite successful. However, the compulsion to be "thorough" was part of why he read so slowly. Eventually, I began to catch glimpses of possible hurts that could have caused his hang-up. Although it was always clear to me that he was an immigrant and English was not his first language, after two hours together he quietly "revealed" to me that he had come to the United States at the age of seven and that English was a second language. While he didn't say much more on the subject, I sensed from listening to him that he might have been remembering children teasing him about past flaws in his English, a hurt that could have led to this compulsive hang-up.

After telling him that I would diagnose more things for him to work on during the next lesson, he became even more dissatisfied. Why? I wasn't keeping him busy enough to feel comfortable. He canceled all future lessons two days later to "engage in another approach," which I am sure involved endless hours of reading and re-reading material. Had I better appreciated the extent to which his hang-up gripped him, I would have kept him busier and he would have eventually improved ... and been happy throughout the process. Hopefully, your investigation center will do a better job of spotting, understanding, and working with hang-ups than I did in this instance.

I am confident that there are a great many other ways to make investigation centers places where the pains of hurts are eased and hang-ups are shed or reduced. We'll explore some of the more promising methods in future lessons.

Lesson Six Assignments

1. What hurts do people you know find difficult to eliminate?

2. How could investigation centers help people reduce such hurts?

3. What other hurts are difficult to reduce?

4. How else might investigation centers help people with these hurts?

5. What hurts would you like to remove?

6. What hang-ups do all such hurts cause?

7. How might investigation centers be helpful in reducing or eliminating such hang-ups?

Lesson Seven:

Have Kingdom Experiences

Jesus answered and said to him,
"Most assuredly, I say to you,
unless one is born again,
he cannot see the kingdom of God."

— John 3:3 (NKJV)

In John 3:3 (NKJV), Jesus addressed Nicodemus, a Pharisee ruler of the Jews who, despite believing that Jesus came from God, was totally puzzled by Jesus' words. Nicodemus didn't realize that, even among those who want to know more about God, more is hidden than revealed about God's Kingdom until the Holy Spirit has entered into someone who has repented, and believed in and accepted Jesus as Lord and Savior. Similarly, most of those who have not yet accepted Jesus have no inkling of the great things that they are missing. Wouldn't it be wonderful if investigation centers could whet at least some nonbelievers' appetites to know more?

About 10 years ago, God provided me with a series of experiences that opened my eyes to how much more supernaturally active He is in the world than I had noticed. Learning about this extremely high level of activity was quite a surprise. After all, I had been a believer and follower of Jesus for over 45 years at that point. How could I have missed so much?

Here's what happened. The Holy Spirit had directed me to launch a global contest to identify and publicize more effective methods for helping nonbelievers decide to accept God's free gift of Salvation, paid for by the crucifixion, and validated by the subsequent resurrection of Jesus. The successful contestants were from a church in Indiana that did a great deal to educate church members about how to witness, including doing so during five minutes of every church activity and service.

In connection with these educational activities, most congregants had prepared written testimonies that described what their lives had been like before accepting Jesus, why they chose to make the commitment to follow Him, and how their lives had improved since then. The resulting testimonies were then published in a paperback, and each person was encouraged to hand out the books to family, friends, neighbors, coworkers, and acquaintances. The approach had two benefits: People who were shy about witnessing discovered a comfortable, interesting way to share testimonies about how believing in and following Jesus had improved their lives, and those who read the stories were spiritually and emotionally moved by what they read. If you would like to learn more about this church and its activities, and to read some of the testimonies, see *Witnessing Made Easy* (Jubilee Worship Center Step by Step Press, 2010) by Bishop Dale P. Combs, Lisa Combs, Jim Barbarossa, Carla Barbarossa, and me.

If I had heard only two or three of these awe-inspiring testimonies in my entire life, gaining such knowledge would have increased my view of how active God is in expanding and improving His Kingdom. However, reading dozens and dozens of awe-inspiring testimonies opened my eyes to their maximum width to see His presence in so many new ways. For example, God had done more miracles in this one congregation than the total of all those miracles that are described in specific detail throughout the entire New Testament!

Having been shocked by how much I had been missing about the frequency and nature of God's supernatural interventions, I asked some other pastors to comment. They related having often heard inspiring, faith-building stories of God's activity during private conversations with their congregants. When I commented that I had never heard any such congregational stories while in church, the pastors agreed that they received a much better sense of God's Kingdom through performing their pastoral duties than did many believers who were mostly engaged in secular pursuits.

Now, if most believers have only a tiny sense of God's actual presence and supernatural activity around them, just imagine how much more limited is the sense of God's Kingdom that nonbelievers have. While it's quite impressive to read inspiring written testimonies, imagine how much more meaning would be gained by hearing directly from those who have had the experiences. Investigation centers are a possible venue for believers to share their compelling testimonies, including any persuasive documentation or other forms of evidence for the truth of what they experienced. Adding such credibility is important. Otherwise some nonbelievers would discount these testimonies as being fictitious. As an example of such limited perceptions, consider that while Thomas Jefferson had great respect for Jesus as a teacher, the third United States president created his own version of the Bible that excluded any references to His miracles, death, or resurrection.

While listening to such believers testify certainly won't be as impressive as watching Jesus raise Lazarus from the dead, I believe that hearing such testimonies would cause many people to spend more time learning about what it means and can be like to believe in and follow Jesus. To increase such exposure, perhaps in-person testimonies could be included, when relevant, as part of the most popular courses at investigation centers.

Here's an example. I fondly remember taking a course seemingly unrelated to faith that taught me a great deal spiritually, even though I had already been a believer for decades. A writer I greatly admired led a course in writing nonfiction. Since I felt called to write, had published a number of articles, and knew that I needed to improve, I was quick to take advantage of what was probably going to be an

51

excellent learning opportunity. I didn't know what to expect during the course except that we would probably be doing some writing.

During one lesson, the writer unexpectedly asked us to use crayons and markers to draw a picture of our spiritual journey. While the exercise felt like something I had done in third grade and I felt awkward because I'm awful at drawing, I did my best. In the course of doing so, I was reminded of the many times that God had miraculously touched my life, creating benefits that could not have come in any other way ... including the several times that He had spared me from death.

Then, the teacher did something wonderfully effective: He asked us to show and explain our pictures to someone else. Having the picture in front of me (as a sort of primitive story board of the sort that script writers use) kept me focused on the key elements of my spiritual journey as I related it.

Having a listener meant I had to turn the events into some sort of narrative. We had been directed to depict the spiritual journey as movement along a road. With that perspective in front of me, putting the events into a story about a journey made it much easier to describe my experiences. In terms of using a storytelling format, it was as easy as if I were just describing a favorite vacation.

The content, of course, meant that I was characterizing events in terms of my beliefs, effectively turning the narrative into a form of spiritual testimony. While I don't know if this effect was the teacher's purpose, the result was certainly quite similar.

After finishing this assignment, I noticed that my fellow students were much more open about their spiritual experiences and beliefs. In the process, I learned quite a bit. For instance, I was struck by one woman relating the joy it had given her to make a pall for the funeral of a good friend who had been a believer. At the time I was more accustomed to viewing funerals as sad occasions, and her comment refocused me on the good part of attending a believer's funeral, that this person was now with God for eternity where there are no tears, hurt, or pain. I could feel my spiritual eyes opened in a way that they had been previously closed, now much more attuned to the eternal consequences of what was happening around me, instead of just focusing on the rather trivial, short-term implications.

Restaging this part of the class could enliven other peoples' spiritual memories and sensitivities in ways that would enable them to see and appreciate more Kingdom experiences. As helpful as such a class would be, the benefits would pale in comparison to providing some powerful, new spiritual experiences. I have often found that guided silent retreats with much of the time spent in contemplation and prayer have greatly increased my focus on God and my ability to understand what He was asking me to do. I've had such wonderful experiences during retreats that were as short as just a few hours and as long as three days. One of the spiritual disciplines that I have found to be highly effective on such occasions is to simply focus on a word or a phrase from a passage of Scripture to which God has drawn my attention. For weeks thereafter, I will find myself mulling over the significance of that word or phrase, as well as what to do in light of my new understanding. In such cases, the Holy Spirit has used God's Word to focus my spirit in a new direction, one that led me to help expand and improve God's Kingdom.

Many people have told me how profoundly they have been affected by serving experiences. I did not fully appreciate what they meant until I was part of a short-term mission in the African nation of Malawi teaching pastors, caregivers, and youth in conjunction with World Relief-Malawi, our church's partner there. I was teaching lessons based on the Bible to pastors. At one point, we experienced the humility that Jesus demonstrated and encouraged at the Last Supper by washing another person's feet. While you might think that doing so would be an unpleasant task on a hot day in a desert land, I found the task to be just the opposite: a work of spiritual celebration that left me happily smiling and feeling lighter than I had in many years. It was as if Jesus wanted me to know a deeper sense of peace than I had previously experienced. Based on the smiles of the pastors who shared the experience, I knew that I was not alone in feeling this way. In fact, there was a long line of pastors and teachers eager to wash even more feet!

While it may be impractical for most people to devote ten days and substantial funds to engage in such a service project, I believe that many of the same kinds of Kingdom experiences can be had by serving in more limited ways closer to home. Many Christian ministries regularly seek volunteers to serve those in need, whether in a homeless shelter or in a nursing home, by delivering food, collecting used clothes, or even helping to build a home. Whenever such experiences include directly serving those whom God wants us to treat as much-beloved brothers and sisters, a true taste will be gained of what God's Kingdom is like.

Initial interest in engaging in such experiences is often limited except among those (often including the young) who feel strongly drawn to provide better opportunities for those in need or who have suffered from injustice. Investigation centers could stimulate interest in such experiences by having those who have previously served describe their experiences during the center's activities, courses, and programs. For instance, Habitat for Humanity (a Christian ministry) has had great success attracting unskilled volunteers who learn to love building homes for poor families after being taught skills that the volunteer might possibly develop and use to gain a paying job in the building industry.

An investigation center could also make it easier to learn about and engage in spiritual experiences within God's Kingdom by consolidating and making available information about activities that are being conducted by local churches, ministries, and other Christian organizations. Such assembled information would usually be much more accessible and complete than what someone could find through individual research on the Internet and by using other readily available sources. Of course, those organizations that needed volunteers would also be helped.

While I could clearly add many other ideas for assisting nonbelievers and believers alike to gain deeply moving spiritual experiences with expanding and improving God's Kingdom, I will leave the subject for now except to note that the work described in Lesson Six for helping people avoid or reduce the pain of hurts and effects of hang-ups could easily be adapted to also provide Kingdom experiences for people going through or helping others with such challenges. In such a context, the spiritual meaning of the experiences could be deepened and made more memorable.

Lesson Seven Assignments

1. What Kingdom experiences have been significant for people you know?

2. How could investigation centers help other people have such experiences?

3. What other Kingdom experiences do you think are important for nonbelievers and believers to have?

4. How might investigation centers increase the availability of such experiences?

5. What Kingdom experiences have been most important in your life?

6. Which of those experiences should others have?

7. How might investigation centers make it more appealing and easier to access any of these Kingdom experiences?

Part Two:

Appealing Islands for Inquiry

I, John, both your brother and companion
in the tribulation and kingdom
and patience of Jesus Christ,
was on the island that is called Patmos
for the word of God and for the testimony of Jesus Christ.

— Revelation 1:9 (NKJV)

In Part Two, we shift to considering what qualities an investigation center should have for best serving the unmet needs described in Part One. While each quality is addressed here in a separate lesson, an investigation center should obviously seek to supply as many of these qualities as possible to those who would benefit.

In doing so, an investigation center should keep in mind the exiled Apostle John's experience while receiving from Jesus the Revelation description of the last days on the lonely island of Patmos. Jesus chose to use that isolated location to unveil and explain some amazing future events, ones that should make anyone eager to learn more about what Jesus offers to those who believe in and follow Him as their Lord and Savior. Jesus' presence made for all of the appeal that John needed to believe and capture this precious information for people in the ages to come.

In making investigation centers more appealing, we should also be sure that Jesus is a central part of the attraction. We should additionally use any special circumstances connected to being at an investigation center to help focus and activate the resulting attention.

We begin in Lesson Eight by looking at the value of convenience for making an investigation center a more desirable and more often-frequented destination. While the island of Patmos was an inconvenient place for John to meet and communicate with other believers, investigation centers should be just the opposite. In this regard, I'm reminded of research I have conducted concerning various kinds of retail outlets. From these investigations, I learned that relatively few people will pass by one outlet of a given type to visit a different one of a similar type. If Burger King is closer, few will go two more blocks to eat at McDonald's. Why? Most people feel that their time is limited and valuable. Consequently, most will accept fewer benefits in exchange for gaining more convenience, especially in saving time. If you doubt that, think about how often you have prepared a gourmet meal to eat by yourself, as compared to just throwing together something simple when eating alone.

In Lesson Nine, we explore being irresistible. Fill a bowl with high quality chocolates and watch the contents disappear. Of course, it's better to be even more irresistible than that: Draw people so strongly that they will gladly make sacrifices to obtain what is available at an investigation center. We'll consider possible ways to create such extreme irresistibility in this lesson.

Lesson Ten shifts our attention to making investigation centers relaxing places to visit. While many people crave more excitement, most adults find, instead, that much of what they do causes tension and stress. After having such experiences, a relaxing environment can be very appealing and soothing. As evidence of the increasing tension and stress some people are undergoing, just consider the rapid expansion of businesses offering various forms of relaxation, such as providing meditation training, therapeutic massages, and comfort-filled experiences.

Making it easy to gain benefits at an investigation center is discussed in Lesson Eleven. In advancing easiness, I'm reminded of the advertisements for a well-known office supply chain that encourage someone to simply press the "easy" button to deal with work needs. The idea is that a customer should let that chain handle all of a business's requirements. Making it easy for visitors to meet their needs at an investigation center can be another way to increase appeal, while incidentally helping offset any excess tension and stress.

After conforming to whatever work environment and activities an employer requires and regularly dealing with still other authorities (such as government officials, children's teachers, and medical practitioners), many people crave flexibility so they can more comfortably engage in necessary activities. Such flexibility might be increased by having a customized schedule, adapting a program's content to better fit personal needs, or just being able to take an unplanned break whenever one is desired. We investigate the most appealing and helpful kinds of flexibility in Lesson Twelve.

It often takes very little to fascinate children. I fondly remember imagining many different circumstances that struck my fancy while playing in empty refrigerator boxes. At another time, a box of shiny mineral samples provided hours of happy dreaming about finding a valuable mine or building a fabulous mineral collection. Reading a children's novel caused me to think about becoming a writer. However, adults usually need more stimulation to become intrigued. The satisfyingly intense experiences of electronic games today are a good example of what can keep an adult avidly repeating an activity again and again. Lesson Thirteen probes how to make investigation centers more intriguing places to visit.

Disneyland can remind us that not everything fun and interesting should be taken seriously. Thus, our reaction to the imaginary characters and places we see in Fantasyland should be quite different from our thoughts while walking and riding among Frontierland's recreations of actual nineteenth-century America. Since an investigation center will be more effective when it provides credible evidence for important truths, we examine how to provide such credibility in Lesson Fourteen.

Finally, Lesson Fifteen looks at transforming investigation centers into more rewarding places to visit. We consider what kinds of rewards, when to provide such rewards, and how rewards should be adjusted to reflect the interests and needs of each visitor.

We proceed now to Lesson Eight: Convenient.

Lesson Eight:

Convenient

Now concerning our brother Apollos,
I strongly urged him to come to you with the brethren,
but he was quite unwilling to come at this time;
however, he will come when he has a convenient time.

— 1 Corinthians 16:12 (NKJV)

In 1 Corinthians 16:12 (NKJV), the Apostle Paul described his personal plans just before ending this most famous of all Biblical fund-raising letters, which was aimed at raising money for Jerusalem's oppressed believers. While doing so, Paul mentioned that the faithful Apollos had decided to put off a trip to the Corinthian church until a convenient time. Since travel was so slow, difficult, and dangerous in those days, Apollos might have intended to travel when the weather was better, there were fewer active robbers, or he could accomplish more by also visiting churches in other cities. Or, Apollos might simply have been tied up with activities that he had already promised to do.

Being mindful of performing Godly activities in more efficient ways is often the right way to go. Unless God calls us to be in a certain place at a specific time, we can often fulfill more of what He is calling us to do by sensibly choosing when and where we go, as well as what we do while there. As many of Jesus' parables encourage, we should always be faithful stewards of the time and resources He provides.

However, making something more convenient does not always increase utilitarian value. Sometimes, the benefit is merely to reduce the need to think or decide. For instance, restaurant servers often describe "today's special" entrees to diners, dishes that earn the restaurant more profit than the regular menu items. Delicious-sounding "special" appetizers may also be mentioned. Such "suggestive selling" will continue during the meal, often including recommendations for desserts, specialty coffees and teas, and possibly even after-dinner liqueurs. If you dislike making food and beverage choices in a restaurant, you may be pleased to receive suggestions that narrow your focus, even though you will probably end up spending and consuming more than other diners. That's one form of convenience.

Investigation centers can similarly improve convenience for visitors by making suggestions, such as ones that help someone to identify ways to gain the most benefit at the center. Otherwise, the sheer number of choices could cause a visitor to turn around and walk out, overwhelmed by the thought of needing to learn about so many things before making a sensible choice. Greeters and those who explain about the center should be well trained and often encouraged to ask questions that will help guide visitors to highly valuable programs and activities.

Even those who like to choose could be overwhelmed at an investigation center that provides many choices. To avoid overloading these people, centers might offer a brief video introducing the center's most valuable activities. After viewing such a video, the visitors could make better-informed decisions about what to do at the center. For those who want to learn more, a short class in what the center offers could be useful. If such a class offers other benefits, such as meeting other visitors over a pleasant meal, some of the visitors would view such an opportunity as being a convenience.

After becoming familiar with a center and its offerings, convenience also requires that visitors be able to quickly find and understand whatever information they seek. For instance, a short video previewing and providing testimonials about a specific course or activity would also make choosing more convenient.

As my speculations concerning Apollos' possible motivations for delaying his departure suggest, convenience can also involve timing. If courses and other activities match any uncommitted times on the schedules of most people who live and work nearby, visitors will more often engage in a convenient program or activity at the center. Interviews with people who come to or live in the area could help pin down the ideal timing for various kinds of offerings. Timing, of course, isn't just about selecting the hour to start. Timing can also relate to picking the better days of the week. While people usually have more leisure time on the weekends than during the work week, more conflicts will also occur on weekends with activities and commitments that involve family, friends, acquaintances, and churches. Naturally, too, the time of the year can affect convenience. Certainly, some kinds of Kingdom experiences will make much more sense when the weather or related activities better fit. Outdoor retreats are going to be more attractive to most people, for example, during mild weather rather than on very hot or cold days. Activities with children will be easier to attend during school vacations.

As the fast-food example in Part Two's introduction suggests, location also affects convenience. If you are next door to an investigation center at the same time as when you know an appealing event is about to start, the convenience involved will greatly increase your inclination to attend. While most of us would like to imagine that we are routinely scheduling our activities to take advantage of such efficiencies, in practice I suspect most people are pretty opportunistic in doing so. In my case, I often add another activity that easily fits into my schedule only after someone brings that activity and its timing to my attention. Frequent e-mail reminders most often help me to do so. If there are two such opportunities occurring at the same time, I will usually attend the first activity I read or hear about. You may have some other method that helps you to accomplish a similar result. As part of any surveys conducted with those who work, shop, and live nearby, be sure to find out how these people like to gain information about activities, courses, events, and experiences they participate in during leisure time. Then, the investigation center should become highly effective in using such communications methods and channels.

In thinking about a location's convenience, it's easy to draw the wrong conclusions. For instance, you might think that you can't move an investigation center (and doing so may well be hard and expensive), but you could certainly set up temporary locations elsewhere that would add essential convenience for some visitors. Think of how many spaces are quite busy during the work day, such as offices and public buildings, but are little used at other times, especially during the weekends. In good weather, investigation centers can be mobile, going to where the potential visitors are. For instance, there are few reasons why some activities, courses, events, and experiences couldn't be taken to many parks, beaches, and play areas. Since many people have long commutes for work or school, investigation centers might take advantage of such times to provide live "call in" programs or podcasts that can be played on portable devices. With the latter approach, exercise time could also be used to gain information from an investigation center.

The location of a center might be perfectly convenient if you are already in the vicinity, but it could also be relatively inaccessible for those who need to make a special trip there. For instance, in Boston many musical and theatrical activities occur at night in the same few blocks. As a result, suburbanites who drive to these locations find parking to be difficult and expensive. Some clever arts organizations recognized and dealt with this problem by contracting with adjacent parking facilities to provide their subscribers with convenient, free parking. In one instance, the organization provides enough parking hours during a visit so that a subscriber can attend two events in the area and also have dinner without paying for parking. When such a visit is extended because of the free parking, two arts organizations can benefit, as do those who attend both events. A restaurant may gain some extra business, as well.

Where providing parking is not practical, an investigation center could, instead, make available free or low-cost, door-to-door transportation. For instance, an arts organization in Boston once offered two tickets, limousine service from your home to a restaurant, a restaurant meal, followed by a ride to the concert and then a ride home for one all-inclusive price. Although I'm sure the limousine company was paid enough for providing this service for doing so to be a profitable activity, the transportation seemed to be free to the person purchasing the concert and dinner package. Using this service was especially convenient on nights when the weather was bad.

I'm not suggesting that investigation centers provide "free" limousines, but certainly those who find it hard to drive, such as elderly people, might find it more convenient if a shuttle bus were available to go to and from their homes and the investigation center. While such service wouldn't be provided at all hours and for all locations, a regular route might be established for people to attend the most compatible activities, courses, events, experiences, and programs. If the cost of the transportation were rolled into a combined price, the travel would certainly feel as if it were free (or at least inexpensive) to the visitors and increase the perception of convenience for some.

Thinking about transportation also brings to mind the opportunity to attract busloads of school children. Most schools have a budget for transportation required to engage in various kinds of off-site learning. Attracting large numbers of students will often require no more than developing programs that harmonize with local curricula and then reaching out to the appropriate administrators and teachers. Museums have long been doing so in connection with introducing youngsters to art, natural history, and science. Investigation centers could easily develop programs that are complementary to school curricula, many of which might be conducted by people whose day jobs formerly involved educational programs for similarly aged young people. Timing would need to match when the school was addressing a parallel subject.

Due to their busy lives, most people find it hard to become involved in activities, courses, and programs that extend over several days, weeks, or months. Consequently, such events should be concentrated into as few occasions as possible. If one visit can accomplish enough, schedule accordingly.

Where it's necessary for an activity, course, or program to continue longer, visitors will appreciate the convenience of being able to "make up" for whatever they miss with video or audio recordings that can be accessed without coming to the investigation center.

In terms of portability, there's very little that must be done at the center. Without cutting back on any programming at the center, look at how to take programs to where people already are, such as in their homes, work places, schools, and churches. While at some locations it won't be permissible to provide information concerning God and His Kingdom, outreach efforts can still be used to attract interest in attending programs at the centers that do contain such information. Keep in mind that it's usually a lot less expensive to send an educator to an audience than it is to take the audience to the educator.

Let's shift our discussion of convenience to consider better using what is learned or experienced. I'm continually struck by how little thought goes into making most programs useful over the long run. For instance, a church may have a handout that summarizes or supplements each sermon or class. After many years, you would be able to cover the floor of a room with such handouts. But how could you ever find the handout you need? Unless you are quite well organized, such materials are soon thrown away or just pile up, never to be looked at again.

I see two possibilities for making what is learned more convenient to access and apply: Provide online libraries from which materials can be easily downloaded, and have knowledgeable volunteers available to answer questions related to the content of past activities, courses, experiences, and programs. If all that an investigation-center provides were designed to encourage and make such access convenient, much greater use would be made of what can be learned. Each application of learning through such resources would also encourage engaging again with the investigation center.

I also suggest that investigation centers use surveys covering a wider geographical area than just where the people live and work who are normally served to identify what kinds of assistance people would like to have that they cannot find anywhere. The surveys might also inquire about how much effort, travel time, and expense individuals would be willing to invest to gain the desired assistance. A good example of a high-value activity is putting together applications for receiving disability payments from Social Security. Such applications aren't often successful unless an attorney assists in their development. Since the size of the potential lifetime income benefit is quite large, those who cannot afford an attorney might be quite willing to do whatever it takes to obtain either low-cost training or direct assistance from legally trained people to improve their applications.

While I am sure that there are many other wonderful ways to make investigation centers and their services more convenient to visitors, I'm confident you now have the general idea of why convenience is such an important quality to emphasize.

Lesson Eight Assignments

1. What forms of convenience have increased the learning and effectiveness of people you know?

2. How could investigation centers become more convenient in ways that would greatly increase how many people learn from them?

3. What other kinds of convenience do you think are important for attracting more learners?

4. How might investigation centers increase the availability of such forms of convenience?

5. How has convenience enabled you to learn and accomplish more than you otherwise would?

6. Which of the forms of convenience that have benefited you should be provided to others?

Lesson Nine:

Irresistible

"And all nations will call you blessed,
For you will be a delightful land,"
Says the LORD of hosts.

— Malachi 3:12 (NKJV)

Two kinds of irresistibility should be differentiated: temptations to do what opposes God's will, of the sort that led Adam and Eve to eat the forbidden fruit in the Garden of Eden; and attractions to do something that will produce good spiritual fruit, such as drawing closer to God and generating eternal benefits by doing works that help expand and improve His Kingdom. In this lesson, we focus on the latter kind of irresistibility. In doing so, we should always keep in mind that there's nothing as irresistible as the opportunity to be with God. Base what an investigation center does on His appeal, and you will maximize irresistibility.

Here's one way to attract people by drawing on God's appeal: Build each program around some aspect of God's nature. Since we are all designed to live in a close relationship with God, providing ways to access more of His qualities will increase desire in each person's spirit to become involved with an investigation center. For instance, God is love. Any number of programs could be offered for how to experience more and deeper love, both with God and with other people. Who wouldn't want to gain that benefit? For nonbelievers, it would make sense to have some programs that include demonstrating Godly love in ways so that more of it could be directly experienced.

Another of God's characteristics is His holiness, being sinless. I suspect that many nonbelievers carry around painful emotional and mental baggage related to their past errors. Believers who haven't yet repented of their sins and mistakes may also be similarly weighed down, much as King David was after sinning with Bathsheba and arranging for her husband to be killed in battle. Almost everyone would like to be free of such pain and discomfort, but many might not appreciate that without seeking to be holy, as He is holy, their futures will contain more of the same kinds of problems, pain, and discomfort. A course in how to live abundantly could, in part, describe ways of relying on faith and repentance to become more holy and thereby to connect more fully with His holiness and gain more peace.

Some people who are quite committed to advancing justice see God as a contributor to injustice. Programs could show how to increase justice by, instead, connecting with God, while varying the approach to reflect whether believers or nonbelievers attend. Part of such a program could include experiences of advancing justice. During such activities, God might choose to intervene and make His presence known in ways that would draw people closer to Him.

While I could certainly outline many more qualities of God and describe how each one could be emphasized and experienced in investigation-center programs to make participation more irresistible, I feel confident that the Holy Spirit will lead you to appreciate what He wants you to do. I shift, instead, now to describing other ways of adding irresistibility while keeping God as the center of the appeal.

In addition to almost everyone wanting to meet God, some mere mortals can also be appealing. People who are well known are usually the best draw, unless they have repulsive reputations. If the celebrity has legitimate knowledge of or a relevant connection to the activity's or program's subject, such involvement is ideal for making an activity or a program more irresistible. If the well-known person is also a believer who will share a relevant testimony, this aspect of the activity or program should be made known, as well.

If a celebrity is already involved in some related, local activity in an ongoing way, it's good to ask if she or he would be willing to spend some time engaging in the investigation center's activities. If the audience for such an activity will exceed the space available at the center, find a bigger venue. I hope you will often have this problem!

Knowledgeable, nonfiction authors can often draw visitors to an event or program, and many of such authors act as if they have too few opportunities to read from, talk about, autograph, and sell their books. Having written a book enhances almost any author's appeal to and credibility with the general public. If the investigation center has determined that the book's contents add significant value, highlighting such value in publicity about the author's involvement can make the program more irresistible.

If one celebrity can draw well, two of equal interest can bring even more people, especially when the celebrities complement one another in providing fuller perspectives concerning the program's subject. For instance, for a program concerning retirement, one celebrity might address how to build a financial nest egg while another celebrity might describe how part of that nest egg can be used to create a more abundant life by expanding and improving God's Kingdom. Naturally, having more than two celebrities can be even better, especially if they will mingle afterward with visitors.

Organizers from nearby centers might share in attracting such celebrities. In doing so, it could eventually become possible to develop a regular tour of celebrities to support and supplement popular programs.

Objects can also attract interest. In making that observation, I'm assuming that most investigation centers will not have substantial security of the sort needed to protect high-value items. However, object-related programs could be held at local sites where adequate security is present, such as museums, art galleries, and retail stores dealing in valuable objects. In many cases, the secure sites involved might value the attendance that such a program could bring, so that the site's managers would promote the event, as well.

Don't assume that scarcity value is the only way to irresistibly attract attention through objects. Sometimes replicas can be effective substitutes for valuables. For instance, a class looking at paintings could distribute post-card reproductions so that each person would have an object to look at more closely and to take home for further examination.

In addition, many people find music to be an irresistible addition to any experience. If there is a musical way to introduce and develop a program, do so. In most cases, recordings of great performances are readily available that can be used to demonstrate whatever points are being made. Simply having a place to perform and an audience may attract the talent for performing some irresistible live music. For instance, student performers from local conservatories and colleges are often interested in playing and singing before live audiences to hone performance skills. Professionals often perform for free, as well, in front of live audiences as part of preparing for a high-profile event.

In the introduction to Part Two, I mentioned chocolate as something that's irresistible to many people. Let's look now at how food and beverages could be part of making a program more irresistible. From studying adult education classes offered in the Boston area, I have been impressed by the growing attendance at cooking courses. At the same time, almost all other types of courses have rapidly declined, including those with substantial practical value, such as ways to start businesses and to make better investments. Cooking programs are so popular that one local adult-education center moved to a new building containing a large number of kitchens so that such classes can be more easily conducted.

What's the appeal? Well, first of all, the instructor is usually a well-known chef who works at a highly regarded restaurant. You have a sort of double celebrity here (chef and restaurant), of the type that we discussed earlier in this lesson. Second, both the instructor and his or her restaurant specifically add to credibility. Many potential students have either dined on the food at such restaurants or have heard good things about having eaten there from people they respect. Third, rarely are these courses about making traditional staples in the usual way, such as macaroni and cheese from a commercially prepared package. Even when a traditional dish is produced at such a course, the ingredients and preparation will be upgraded to create a more desirable (a more irresistible, as it were) alternative. When the dish is based on a nontraditional cuisine for a student, understanding may be established that will make it possible to prepare a great many more dishes requiring some of the same methods and ingredients. Fourth, students acquire the recipes and the experience necessary to recreate the dishes. Consequently, the program seems quite inexpensive in terms of the number of times that the results might be recreated. Fifth, many people who attend want to have a better reputation for cooking. As a result, they are looking forward to "amazing" family and friends with what they provide in the future, a benefit these attendees may see as being priceless. Sixth, the instructor brings all the ingredients, greatly reducing the amount of time involved in trying out a new way of cooking. Seventh, in many cases the instructor also preps the ingredients before the class so that the amount of work done by students is quite small. Eighth, since the class is probably well attended, there's a chance to become acquainted with several others in a friendly environment. After such an encounter, two students might decide to teach each other recipes they have learned during other courses. Ninth, such programs often include wine, which can convert the learning into something more like a social occasion. Value is often increased by a vintner or distributor having provided some wine to encourage future purchases. Tenth, and perhaps most important for sensory enjoyment, the students eat the food that has been prepared. So there's the experience of having a great meal in the company of similarly interested people. Few people would find such an experience to be less than appealing.

Eleventh, the chef is usually not providing the course to earn money from teaching, but rather as a promotional activity for attracting diners, take-out customers, and catering business. So the chef will usually go out of her or his way to be charming, entertaining, and interesting. If the increase in future student restaurant usage is expected to be great enough, the chef may provide the ingredients at no charge. When that happens, the price paid by participants will be a tiny fraction of the cost, with the fee probably just covering space costs, and administrative and marketing expenditures. Twelfth, how could God become part of the experience? The dishes offered might be ones related to something that occurred in the Bible, such as the Last Supper. Or the ingredients could be ones that were commonly used in Biblical times, allowing opportunities to connect a Bible story to the food experience. Alternatively, the menu could be one suitable for serving on Christmas or Easter.

I have just provided this extensive example to help you better appreciate how combining many appealing elements can greatly improve irresistibility. Before leaving this subject, let me provide a cautionary tale of the way that one organization applied this approach ... and then took it in the wrong direction.

Instead of having one class for which a fee was charged, this organization developed a fund-raising event: A donation to the organization entitled the donor to attend a dinner. Beverages were donated by organizations that manufactured or distributed them. Chefs from the best nearby restaurants were invited to compete in preparing several dishes. Those with the best food were then selected to do so in a hotel ballroom (usually over hot plates). The chefs provided all of the ingredients at no charge. So the organization had no expenses other than for promoting the event, and renting and decorating the ballroom. Donors paid about the price of an individual meal, beverages, and tips at such an individual restaurant. However, the donors were able to eat and drink an unlimited amount, much as they might at a buffet, from dozens of restaurants, thus benefiting from having many more choices and a larger quantity of food than would normally occur at one meal. In addition, the cost of attending the event was reduced by donors receiving a tax deduction equal to a portion of the amount paid.

You might be thinking that such tickets would sell out years in advance. Let me share a little secret: This organization then made a large mistake by extending the evenings to include many tiresome speeches and then deliberately building peer pressure for donors to give large sums at the event. As a result, only those who already planned to donate a substantial amount of money or who felt obligated to the event's organizers were willing to go. Most people attended once, and then avoided returning.

Don't waste whatever irresistibility you create by adding unpleasant elements. Be like the chefs who donated the food at the donor dinner: They treated everyone well and their only "sales pitch" was to have cards available on their tables to remind donors of their restaurants. As a result, many new diners probably came to their restaurants, creating at least some relationships that may well have continued.

We all have different ideas about what is irresistible. I am sure your investigation center will be sensitive to adding just the right elements to your programs ... and nothing else.

Lesson Nine Assignments

1. What forms of irresistibility have increased the learning and effectiveness of people you know?

2. How could investigation centers become more irresistible in ways that would greatly increase how many people learn from them?

3. What other kinds of irresistibility do you think can attract more learners?

4. How might investigation centers increase the availability of such irresistible qualities?

5. How has irresistible attraction enabled you to learn and accomplish more than you otherwise would?

6. Which of the forms of irresistibility that attracted you to learn and accomplish more should be provided to others?

Lesson Ten:

Relaxed

"Peace I leave with you, My peace I give to you;
not as the world gives do I give to you.
Let not your heart be troubled,
neither let it be afraid."

— John 14:27 (NKJV)

"Relaxed" isn't a word that you'll find in most Bible translations. In searching for a relevant verse to share with you, I looked for "untroubled." When that word didn't turn up in the New King James Version, I tried "not troubled" and found several verses. Of those, I think that John 14:27 (NKJV) best captures what Jesus intended, a peace so complete that it eliminates feeling troubled, as well as being afraid. Surely, anyone would feel relaxed while experiencing such peace.

A troubled heart can come from many sources: sins that haven't been repented, a mistake with painful consequences, concerns about the future, and feeling conflicted about what to do. Jesus came, died, and rose again to eliminate these and other causes of troubled hearts. Because of His sacrifice, any sins can be cleansed by His precious blood, enabling a believer who genuinely repents to have a fresh start. Even if a mistake isn't a sin, Jesus will forgive that, too. In fact, He already has. Jesus has told us that if we focus on Him and His Kingdom, our needs will be met (Matthew 6:33, NKJV). We should not be concerned about the future. If we don't know what to do, we should ask for guidance in prayer, study the Scriptures to find what is commanded, and ask knowledgeable, Godly people for help to think through our choices. Through these and other means, He will reveal the right choice. Realizing that we have such good assistance should make anyone breathe easier and sleep better.

By contrast, fear comes from the enemy who is in the world. In a relationship with God, there is no reason to fear. God has only our best interests in His heart. While He may provide challenges and tests to build our faith, grow us spiritually, and make us more effective for His Kingdom, the result will mean that we can better withstand whatever else comes our way. While God won't take away dangers and tribulations, He will be with us while we encounter them to protect, guide, and encourage us. To better appreciate what He will do, think about what Psalm 23 (NKJV) says about life with God.

While in contact with an investigation center, everyone should clearly receive gentle, considerate treatment. Every effort should be made to prepare in advance so that what is said and the way meaning is conveyed will leave visitors feeling relaxed about what is happening, as well as about what might follow. For instance, care should be taken to choose investigation-center locations that seem and are safe, open, friendly, and comfortable. If you would like some ideas for how to do so, get help from an interior designer. As I walk around various public buildings, I'm often struck by how inviting their interiors are. Clearly, the impressions I've developed on such occasions were intended by someone who appreciated how to help people relax. Interestingly, some of these interiors are so nicely done that they make even somewhat sketchy outside areas seem to be relatively benign.

How can interior spaces encourage such responses? Well, there are usually lots of open areas, ones that are often quite large. Consequently, someone can enter and not feel crowded. Even if a person wants to sit or stand while talking to six friends, there's still plenty of uncrowded space to do so. In addition, there are often large, vibrant plants, providing a sense of being a little in nature. The spaces usually feature warm colors that are nicely subdued. You can often find a mural or other playful element adorning the walls to indicate that there is nothing "stuffy" going on here. Once inside, you will notice music playing in the background at just the right volume for helping set a pleasant mood. Many areas have an adjacent or nearby café or coffee bar that generates pleasant coffee or chocolate aromas. The furniture is often upholstered in rich fabrics or leather that just begs to be touched. Staff members wear casual, but tasteful, clothing and use friendly body language while interacting with anyone.

After having presented Godly perspectives in such an environment, what else can an investigation center do to relax visitors? First and foremost, be sure everyone knows that God wants them to be relaxed. While many nonbelievers might not be attracted to a class or a program focused on God's preference for eliminating troubled hearts and fears, His perspective needs to be learned by everyone. Instructors of programs about being relaxed might share personal testimonies about how God relieved them of distressed hearts and fear. Such testimonies could be held in reserve until questions are asked about how the instructor has handled difficult situations that would leave most people feeling frazzled. While it would be nice to think that all believers are already highly aware of and acting in accordance with such Godly desire to banish troubled hearts and fears, undoubtedly there are some believers who also need help in this regard. I make this observation due to how often I meet believers who live in great fear of all kinds of things, often even of risks that seldom result in harm, such as unusual kinds of accidents.

I often work with people who become so tense during school, admissions, and professional examinations that their normally effective and efficient minds stop working well. I find that such people are often helped by refocusing from the thought that makes them tense or afraid to something that they associate with being relaxed. For instance, a believer might recite the words "God's love" aloud or mentally, until a sense of that love suffuses every part of the body. For each person, a different word or phrase will help the most. If a believer's focus can be tied to God, I feel that relaxation will be greater. Someone who doesn't yet have a sense of God's love might read a brief Bible passage that tells a relevant story, such as Jesus' parables of the Prodigal Son and the Good Samaritan.

Changing someone's posture or body position can also be relaxing. I often suggest that someone sit or stand in the same way as when he or she last felt completely relaxed and fully confident. I watch the person's eyes until I see them focused internally on recalling such an experience. As they do, muscles relax, limbs droop, and peace breaks out on the face. Whenever such changes stop, I check to see if total relaxation and confidence are being expressed. If not, I simply ask the person to feel the same way as she or he did before, but more completely. After a few such encouragements, the individual will eventually appear to be totally relaxed and confident.

Of course, in such a state few people are going to want to do much other than enjoy feeling that way. As soon as they return to doing normal activities, tension and fear will creep back into their minds, moods, and bodies. To overcome this tendency, I encourage people to check their own physiologies from time to time and then to return to the ideal physical position whenever they have left it. By doing so, they gradually build the relaxing habit of always being in a better physiology and related emotional state.

Mere concentration (such as helps while doing a difficult task or taking a test) can be so tiring that people who have been worn out by this focus often assume that concentrating while being relaxed is impossible. Fortunately, the reality is a great deal better than this assumption.

Here are some ways to combine concentration and relaxation. First, increase energy by taking a break for about 45 seconds, every 25 or so minutes. While doing so, look at a distant point, stretch, do anything to feel more comfortable, and return to the ideal physiology. Doing this routine builds energy, but, more importantly, also usually increases attention to near optimal levels.

Let's now imagine an investigation-center class or activity. Whoever leads the engagement should provide ways to help visitors become and remain relaxed. For instance, the environment should be conducive to relaxation in every possible way, from the space to the lighting to the seating. Directions for relaxing should be given at the beginning and repeated at regular intervals, so that attention will become and remain high. For groups of believers, Bible verses should be shared before praying for God to take away any uneasiness and fear. Sharing information and knowledge should mostly be done as Jesus did, through stories that eloquently transmit what should be thought and done in ways that get the point across, but without creating anxiety for those who want to improve. Activities should shed stress and worries. Program pacing should feel comfortable and unforced. Discussions and interactions of all sorts should be done in the most peaceful way possible, begging pardon in advance for doing anything that disturbs peace. Finally, it will be good to have an observer watching the bodies of those involved for any signs that peace is being disturbed. Whenever the relaxed state has been disrupted, the observer should immediately stop and talk calmly about whatever has just upset one or more people.

Even with such an observer present, it's good to regularly ask people if they feel relaxed. Doing so will reinforce that the center's purpose is, in part, to promote relaxed experiences. As a result, visitors will be more likely to point out when something has stressed them.

Keep in mind that it's stressful for most adults just to feel that they are having difficulties while learning or doing something new. Be sure to set low expectations for visitors so that they will avoid seeing their progress as below what should be achieved.

Also be aware that relaxation is a response to different inputs, depending on an individual's prior experiences and the culture from which he or she comes. Be up-front in asking for advice about how to operate in a more relaxed manner, especially when what you had intended to be relaxing hasn't worked well. For example, some people cannot imagine feeling relaxed without being physically active.

Others would feel as if such activity would just wear them out and be a distraction. In describing activities, be clear whether people will be sedentary or active. If an activity attracts people who vary in such preferences, consider ways to split the group so that both activity and inactivity fit well with the rest of the program. You might find it helpful to have sub-leaders vary the program accordingly.

I've mentioned before the idea of surveying people about what would bring them to a center. Keep in mind it's also important to ask questions of those who are involved in activities, courses, events, and programs about how they prefer to learn and apply what they study. In doing so, be flexible in adjusting to what you hear.

In future lessons, I will have more to say concerning relaxation, but we'll draw this subject to a close for now.

Lesson Ten Assignments

1. How do people you know become more relaxed while trying new things and learning?

2. How could investigation centers become more relaxed in ways that would greatly increase how many people learn?

3. What other ways of relaxing people do you think can attract more learners?

4. How might investigation centers add helpful kinds of relaxation that are seldom available?

5. How has becoming and remaining relaxed enabled you to learn and accomplish more than you otherwise would?

6. Which of the forms of becoming and remaining relaxed that helped you to learn and achieve more should be provided to others?

Lesson Eleven:

Easy

"Come to Me, all you *who labor and are heavy laden,*
and I will give you rest.
Take My yoke upon you and learn from Me,
for I am gentle and lowly in heart,
and you will find rest for your souls.
For My yoke is easy and My burden is light."

— Matthew 11:28-30 (NKJV)

If you speak to most believers about why they were once reluctant to accept Jesus as Lord and Savior, concern about being directed to take on difficult tasks that an individual saw as daunting is a common reason that is given. For instance, someone might have been concerned that God would require serving as a missionary in rural Africa. Of the people I've known who once had such concerns, I don't recall any who were, in fact, later told by God to make a move that they viewed at the time as being anything other than a blessing.

Before accepting Jesus as Lord, such concerns are often based in ignorance about who Jesus is and what He stands for. For instance, in considering such concerns about difficult tasks, we can see that the possibilities raised by such concerns are at odds with what Jesus had to say in Matthew 11:28-30 (NKJV).

Yet, some people (me included) have been asked by God to take on what initially seemed to be impossible tasks. How does having such an experience relate to His words?

Here's my interpretation based on my personal experiences. Before accepting Jesus as Lord and Savior, we always have the dual burdens of first finding what is best to do and then of relying solely on our own resources to make the choice work. When problems arise (as they always do), we are mostly on our own to deal with them, as well. Taking on so much perfectly describes to me an experience of laboring while carrying heavy burdens.

What is it like, by contrast, to take on some "impossible" task for Jesus? To do so, I first needed to strengthen and better inform my faith. After doing that, I didn't either have to work any harder or to feel weighed down by the task. Instead, well-informed faith taught me to begin by just doing what only I could do and then relying on Jesus to accomplish the rest. To me, such teamwork felt like having the ability to do *anything* that was in His will. Jesus and I were both carrying a very heavy weight, but He was doing all of the heavy lifting. I was just lifting the little that I could carry without being strained. My physical burden might have been near to the limits of my capabilities at times, but while doing so my mind, emotions, and spirit always felt as light as a single feather.

So the easiness described in this lesson isn't the same as leaning back on a hot summer's day in a reclining chair under air conditioning while sipping icy lemonade. Instead, this easiness involves releasing concerns, doubts, and difficulties to the One who can handle them and wants to do so because He loves you so much.

Jesus must often shake His head in wonder when we forget this basic lesson, often due to wanting to accomplish our idea of desirable "results" before He wants us to do so. When we try to get ahead of Jesus, He graciously stands aside while we plug away at whatever kinds of efforts we want to do during long, frustrating days, weeks, months, and even years of work. Of course, Jesus knows that what we are doing is often going to be a waste of time, resources, and effort. In fact, our "supreme" efforts may actually delay what would otherwise occur. He has a better way, but He knows that sometimes we have to engage in futile efforts on our own before we fully appreciate having Him take charge. Whenever we get tired of doing such foolish things in our own strength, we can ask Jesus to bear the burden and He will.

His promise means a great deal more than the advertising slogan of the office supplies chain about making work easier for businesses by providing any needed materials. While anyone can make such a promise, only Jesus can deliver the results in any area of life.

Making life easier for visitors is an important benefit for an investigation center to provide. Many people who are not walking with God have gotten tangled up in such horrible messes that they don't see any way to recover from them. I suspect that having such difficulties will drive some people to an investigation center as a last resort, not realizing that God is the only resource they need.

God can take away the causes or the effects of all the messes in a few seconds, should such a change fit with His purposes. Here's an example. Think about the demon-filled man described in Mark 5 (NKJV) who had been cutting himself with stones in the cemetery. The poor fellow had been so crazed by a legion of demons that he could not be restrained. Jesus sent all the demons into a nearby herd of pigs, and the man was immediately restored to sanity and peacefulness. In addition to helping the man, Jesus also accomplished a great deal for the Kingdom by directing him to tell his story to others, spreading awareness of Jesus' supernatural powers and how the demons had identified Him as the Son of God.

While God may not immediately take away all of the difficulties that someone has gotten into, He would certainly like to quickly remove any burdens from a person's mind and spirit. To facilitate such a result, a center should always have someone either present or quickly available by telephone to counsel those who are downcast. Those who once created horrible messes that God cleaned up will be best for serving in this role. If such counselors can also carry their responsibilities lightly, a discouraged visitor may more easily be able to appreciate that life's burdens can become bearable.

After being sure to manifest what Jesus said about experiencing life with Him, an investigation center should also review its processes to ensure they are as simple, understandable, and comfortable as possible. During such a review, the focus should be on making everything visitors do trouble free. For instance, unless expensive, perishable materials are needed for participating in an activity or a class, it would be best if a visitor could become involved simply by indicating the desire to attend, such a notification only serving the purpose of enabling communications about proper preparation and how to make up for anything that has been missed. Although so far I have not discussed how to pay for a center's costs, the more that someone can become initially involved without paying anything, the better the center will probably provide for visitors, especially first-time ones. I make this suggestion because part of making a mess out one's life usually means having few financial resources and even fewer ways to obtain them. When that is the case, people who most need help may well be those who can least afford to make even token payments.

Some processes cannot be made any simpler and less burdensome than they are. However, in those cases the ease that someone experiences can be greatly increased by another person doing whatever is required. For instance, here's how getting started at an investigation center might be experienced. A volunteer or staff member at the center would greet a visitor, ask what the visitor would like to drink or eat, provide what is requested, and sit down in a comfortable, private place to answer questions and explain about the center. During a pleasant conversation, the visitor might express interest in a certain program. The staff member or volunteer would open up a portable computer and play a video describing the program that includes some comments by those who lead it as well as observations by those who have taken it. If the visitor expresses an interest in learning more, the center representative would reach someone on the phone to expand on what had just been shown. Such a conversation might continue by exploring a variety of ways for the visitor to become involved at the center until an appropriate activity, class, course, experience, event, or program was selected. At that point, the representative would do whatever was required to prepare the visitor for engaging in the selection, as well as perform any administrative tasks (such as registration). Before leaving the center, the visitor would be asked if she or he wanted to meet someone who would be attending, including the class or event leader. If interest was expressed, the representative would arrange a time to talk and make the necessary introductions. With the visitor's permission, a photograph of him or her would be put into the archives so that those leading the class or event would recognize and be able to welcome the visitor by name at the first face-to-face meeting. Before the visitor left, the representative would also politely inquire if there are any things for which the visitor would like to have prayers made. If yes, permission would be requested to then do the first prayer aloud together.

At the initial occasion for engaging in the selection, the visitor would be joined by someone whose assignment would be to ensure that the visitor has a good experience. Doing so might involve introducing the visitor to other people there, learning more about what the visitor hopes to gain, and sharing any information obtained with the program leader. During casual conversation, the visitor's comments and questions would be used to suggest ways to gain more benefits from the selection, as well as other ways to be helped by the center. Ideally, the two people would then find something else that they would like to do together and schedule doing so before this occasion ended.

If for some reason the visitor didn't want to have such help, the representative would quickly identify that preference and ask if the visitor would like to be left alone. If that's the answer, the information would be captured so that the visitor wouldn't receive any more friendly contacts in the future than were desired.

If the two people hit it off, the representative would make it a point to stay in touch with the visitor to suggest activities and events that could be done together until such time as the visitor develops her or his own circle of contacts. Before withdrawing from being the visitor's helper, there should be a friendly conversation about how the visitor would like to have the center assist in the future so that all such interactions would feel easy and comfortable.

Throughout every contact with a visitor, staff and volunteers at the center should be sensitive to noticing the need for special support. Many people may arrive bravely putting on a smiling face concerning bad situations. Inside, they might be ready to totally break down. If there's any sense that special support would be valuable, the visitor should be encouraged to engage in making such a connection.

While I'm sure that there are many more things that would make an investigation center easy for visitors, let's leave the subject for now.

Lesson Eleven Assignments

1. What makes trying something new and learning easier for people you know?

2. How could investigation centers make visitor experiences easier in ways that would greatly increase how many people learn?

3. What other ways of being easy do you think could attract more learners?

4. How might investigation centers add helpful forms of being easy that are seldom available?

5. How has being easy enabled you to learn and accomplish more than you otherwise would?

6. Which of the forms of being easy that helped you to learn and achieve more should be provided to others?

Lesson Twelve:

Flexible

But He is unique, and who can make Him change?
And whatever His soul desires, that He does.

— Job 23:13 (NKJV)

In Job 23:13 (NKJV), Job first describes God before relating his reactions to God's nature in the rest of the chapter. Whenever I read this chapter, I'm also reminded that God made each person to be unique, undoubtedly as an expression of His own, unique nature. There is a difference, however, in what kinds of uniqueness are involved. While God is immutable, mere humans can and do change. In the process, we can be unique in different (and in hopefully more Godly) ways throughout life. Despite the potential to be flexible in positive ways, people find some kinds of changes to be harder than others; and some changes can even be counterproductive, at least in the near term.

Here's an example of what I mean. Someone who is either right- or left-handed will find it initially difficult to conduct activities as well solely with the other hand. Despite this initial difficulty, there can be long-term benefits from developing similar skill in using each hand: Some important tasks will become quite a bit easier or might even be accomplished much better.

In recent years, scientists have been learning more about how the brain and nervous system function. While it was once believed that brains could not add new cells, we now know that brain cells can be generated throughout someone's life. In addition, new neural connections can be made in the brain at any time, which means that new learning can occur over a lifetime.

People who solely studied human behavior could have deduced such characteristics much earlier. For instance, there are numerous cases of someone losing the ability to function in a certain way after severe injury or illness affected the brain or nervous system, but then the person later learned from scratch what to do so that functionality was completely restored. That's the basis of much physical therapy, for example.

One dimension of being human is immutable: the consequences of accepting the free gift of God's Salvation. The Bible tells us that once we accept Jesus as Lord and Savior, through the Holy Spirit the process begins of transforming us into a person who is more like Christ. These changes begin to occur because the Holy Spirit comes to live within us. A second consequence of this decision is that our Salvation is permanent. We are going to live and be with God for all eternity.

Consider that such transformations occur even among new believers who were once uninterested in God, did not even believe that God exists, or had been angry with God. Accomplishing so much change is an indication of the remarkable flexibility that God has built into each one of us. Looking back on their prior lives, many believers have a difficult time understanding how they could have ever thought and behaved the way they did before.

So there's a tension between people finding many changes hard to make while having quite a remarkable, life-long capacity to make major changes ... especially in spiritual improvements through the Holy Spirit's influence. Investigation centers need to be extremely aware of and sensitive to this tension. In better providing for visitors, flexibility will be an essential quality for doing so.

Let me use an example to explain why flexibility is so important. I recently had a conversation with two people who had kindly offered to help me with leading and teaching a discipleship course. To accomplish the most, we had each learned a variety of methods that could be applied to this course. In the past, we had been able to apply extensive preparation time in an empty meeting room to utilize more of these methods. In this conversation, however, we realized that there would be very little time to do such preparations, due to another course being held in the same room until a few minutes before this course would start.

Our initial reaction was to feel that we wouldn't be able to use very many of these methods. However, the Holy Spirit encouraged each of us to do the best possible job. We realized that we needed to consider other ways of applying these methods. One man thought of a way to test if using simpler forms of these methods would make it possible to apply more of them. I began thinking about how having more helpers could make it possible for more to be accomplished in a short amount of time by reducing how much each person had to do. Our female teammate kept reminding us to look to God for guidance, expressing hope that He would reveal solutions. Empowered by such thoughts, we adopted flexibility in looking at choices, flexibility that left us feeling good. As one indication of flexibility's value, this man and woman expressed concern that they might have to miss an occasional class. I indicated that I was prepared to adjust to that. I simply asked that they let me know in advance. Although we were speaking on the telephone, I could almost tangibly feel my indication of being flexible relieving some tension and stress in them.

As I thought about that experience, I realized that respect, caring, and love underlie willing flexibility. Let me describe two ways of handling a situation to demonstrate what I mean. A well-known luxury hotel chain has an operating philosophy requiring anyone working there to stop whatever task is going on to fix any problem that has been observed or encountered. For instance, a guest might be looking for the restroom in the lobby, glancing around while wearing a puzzled expression. In such a circumstance, a staff member is told to inquire if the guest needs help. Rather than simply provide directions, the staff member is then to walk the guest to the restroom and after arriving to inquire if anything else is needed. Clearly, the intent behind this approach is to make guests feel important and deserving of attention. Ego-driven people might enjoy receiving such attention.

By contrast, I don't particularly want someone to walk me to the restroom. It feels awkward to me. I know because I've had this experience. It felt to me a bit like when my father would take me to a restroom just after I had been toilet trained. Unless I am unlikely to locate the restroom I would rather that someone just told me how to get there.

A flexible approach would mean, instead, that staff members at this hotel chain would adapt their actions and speech to match the preferences of the individual, rather than always providing the most assistance. Maximizing what is done can actually be patronizing. I often see this point demonstrated by interactions with people who have a few physical difficulties while getting around. Perhaps they are in a wheelchair, using a walker, or wielding a white cane. Many able people will rush unbidden to open doors, grab any coats or packages being carried, take an arm while crossing the street, or otherwise treat the individual as being helpless.

When I have taken a moment to first ask those with a few physical difficulties if they would like any assistance, I can't remember any of them saying "yes." Using aids to get around is more often a sign of someone's fierce independence, rather than being a sign of wanting help. As this example demonstrates, we should always ask for what a person wants before doing anything. When we do, we express flexibility that can increase the encountered person's worth in his or her own eyes, as well as in our own. In the process, the possibility of sharing God's love is created.

While it's certainly good to encourage flexibility at an investigation center, what should the center be flexible about? The simple answer is "everything." However, such an answer probably doesn't help you very much.

Let's look at some kinds of flexibility that are likely to be important. Most people rely more on some senses than on others to absorb new information and to apply it. While vision plays some role in learning for almost everyone who isn't blind, many people also want to "hear" and "feel" more of what's involved than they want to "see" anything. Despite such preferences, many learning environments only emphasize seeing. Even those who primarily rely on sight for learning will also gain a deeper appreciation of what's going on if they can also hear, touch, feel, and smell in relevant ways.

In addition, most people learn much better if they have opportunities to apply new information and learning in some practical way. If each person has a different potential use for what has been studied, a program that offers only one way to apply its content may well be ineffective for almost everyone. Instead, flexibility should be built into how first applications are experienced during a program.

In today's pluralistic society, no one should assume that programs should only be conducted in English. There may be a need for simultaneous translations into Spanish, Chinese, Korean, or any of a number of other languages. If there are enough people who only know the same non-English language, whole programs should be offered just in that language. As a result, volunteers and staff members need to have a way to relate to visitors who know little or no English. Once again, having a way to quickly contact those who can translate is important. Naturally, most of such work will have to be done over a speakerphone feature so that the visitor and the people at the center can each hear what the translator is saying.

Different cultural norms will also need to be respected. Strict Muslims, for instance, aren't going to be involved in a place where the dress and behavior aren't pretty conservative relative to the typical American gathering. If Muslims are attending programs that extend over several hours, there may be a need for prayer breaks and a place for prayer rugs to be unrolled.

Certain cultures don't favor men and women sitting together in public, even if they are married. Such norms would need to be honored or certain people will not be helped. Obviously, accommodating such cultural observations will require both knowledge of these norms and flexibility in adjusting to them by the center.

There are even more subtle issues that are usually ignored on a day-to-day basis. Experts estimate that 40 percent of Americans are functionally illiterate. If a program relies heavily on people reading, how will illiterate people learn? Many older people cannot hear well. Such individuals may need devices that amplify sound to have any idea of what's going on.

While there are an almost unlimited number of things to consider being flexible about, we can rely on the Holy Spirit and being genuinely interested in helping other people to aid us in gaining the information we need to provide the right adjustments. As we do, keep in mind that we should do so as fallible human representatives of a loving, perfect God.

It's time to move on to our next topic, making investigation centers intriguing.

Lesson Twelve Assignments

1. How has flexibility assisted people you know to try something new and learn valuable lessons?

2. How could investigation centers be flexible in ways that would greatly increase how many people learn?

3. What other ways of being flexible do you think could attract more learners?

4. How might investigation centers be improved by adding helpful flexibility that is seldom available?

5. How has flexibility enabled you to learn and accomplish more than you otherwise would have?

6. Which of the ways of being flexible that helped you to learn and achieve more should be provided to others?

Lesson Thirteen:

Intriguing

In that day the Branch of the LORD
shall be beautiful and glorious;
And the fruit of the earth
shall be excellent and appealing
For those of Israel who have escaped.

— Isaiah 4:2 (NKJV)

"Intriguing" doesn't appear in most Bible translations. In choosing this quality for an investigation center, I mean to convey being mentally appealing in a way that causes us to dwell on the person or object, thereby gaining an appreciation for many more aspects of the qualities or potential of what is being contemplated. A good visual analogy is looking at a crystal prism that can cast rainbow colors in an almost infinite number of ways by being rotated at different distances from a variety of colored and clear light sources. While examining what is projected, our minds perceive different references, as well as other ideas for creating unique views. Unless other matters are pressing, a few seconds of idle examination can easily stretch into spending many minutes, or even hours, without our being aware of how much time has passed.

Isaiah 4:2 (NKJV) appears following Isaiah's prophecy that the Israelites would be conquered and carried off by the Babylonians. While some read this verse as only a continuation of the prophecy,

Christians often see the reference to the "Branch of the LORD" as meaning the second coming of Jesus. As a result, what follows in the verse can also be seen as a description of restoring Zion after Judgment Day. The book of Revelation describes Jesus as returning then in all of His glory, which could certainly be considered "beautiful and glorious," as this verse from Isaiah indicates. We also know from Revelation that Jesus will bring a new heaven and a new Earth then. Won't the new Earth bring forth what is excellent and appealing? It's hard to imagine otherwise. Wouldn't it be great if potential visitors could find an encounter with an investigation center to be similarly appealing? Well, at least we can move in that direction.

Writing about this subject reminds me of an experience I had in 1978. Mitchell and Company had just moved into its first office in a storefront. Wanting to make the premises more appealing, we had the wooden walls refinished, brought in some plants, and rented new furniture. Still, the place looked a bit incomplete. Fortunately, an art dealer I knew had just acquired new pieces. Since all these works were inexpensive, I bought enough to put an interesting one on each wall.

Each artwork was intended to provoke thought. As an example, one print showed people happily playing in a garden under which, unknown to them, lay buried an enormous dinosaur skeleton. That print caused me to wonder what important things I was ignoring. Another print looked like a railroad-crossing sign in terms of its shape and colors, but on it there were words that referred to various kinds of crossings (such as from one side of the United States to the other, and from life to death). I'm sure you get the idea about how these art works could stimulate thoughts beyond considering their obvious representations.

Because the office was located at street level with windows all around, anyone could easily peer in. Occasionally, someone would stop and take a long glance. I didn't think much about this visibility until early one evening when a woman looked inside with her face scrunched up against a window. She paid no attention to me while I observed her. She would first look unblinkingly at one piece of art, and then turn her face, still pressed against the window, towards a different one. This "art tour" lasted for about 20 minutes. Finally, she pulled her face away from the window, and I could see her normal appearance. I was shocked to recognize Julia Child, a local celebrity who worked as a television chef and was the author of a highly admired book about French cooking.

As I reflected on her extended observations of the artworks, I began to realize that images can become launching pads for extensive mental stimulation of a sort that I had not often engaged in. Subsequently, I used that insight to develop an art collection containing new works with ambiguous images that more significantly stimulated viewers to imaginatively determine what was going on and what it meant. I later provided tours of my art collection to help clients realize that the surface meaning of things can be quite different from their fully considered significance. Subsequent to those tours, I also began taking clients to museums where I explained some of the more difficult works that they had not previously understood. Many happy hours followed as their minds were unlocked to possibilities that intrigued them.

At this point, you may be wondering how I distinguish being "intriguing" from being "irresistible." While the latter is essential for attracting the most people to an information center, the quality of being intriguing is equally essential for helping visitors gain the most benefit from their experiences at the center. In the process of encountering an irresistible attraction, some of such people will then become intrigued by the possibilities of what else they might learn at a center and want to return often to engage with the center in many more ways.

While obviously the décor and furnishings of investigation centers can play the role of "conversation pieces" in being icebreakers among strangers, I think it's even more important for the content of whatever is done by the center to play the same role. Let me explain. The content of any activity, class, course, event, experience, or program has to be kept as simple as possible, or many people will be confused and possibly turned off. However, being simple enough doesn't mean that something has to be simple-minded. Instead, layers of meaning can be made available, layers that can be grasped in a variety of ways by those with different kinds and amounts of experience in, perception concerning, and interest in a subject.

Here's an example. Imagine a course that highlights the main attributes of the world's most popular faiths. Each topic should be approached with complete respect. Otherwise, there would be a crippling lack of credibility concerning the accuracy of what was said. Many people would stop with accomplishing such a result. However, the treatment could become more intriguing by including in each topic a credible presentation of some positive aspect of that faith that even those who observe the faith don't often appreciate. In this way, even someone of that faith could learn from the encounter. Another way to make such material more intriguing is by using a format that will make it easier for visitors to compare the information provided about one faith with the material about a different one. By doing so, some visitors could more effectively apply the information to mull over what those differences might mean. Further, each characterization of a faith might also be constructed in such a way that those who want to dig deeper would know where to go and what to do. Such a result might be accomplished by including specific references to that faith's writings, historical sources, or archeological evidence, as well as to commentaries by highly regarded, impartial observers. Finally, the context for such a course might be supplied in terms of an intriguing analogy or a metaphor, so that such contextual references could lead visitors to gain new insights into what is or is not present in each faith.

Ambiguity can also be an excellent basis for making something more intriguing. If something looks like one thing, yet is also something else, we are going to spend more time looking at and thinking about what we've seen. Consider the often-viewed drawing that contains both the image of a beautiful young woman and the silhouette of an aged woman's face. Our minds flip from first one image to the other. Then, we start to ponder how single lines in the drawing help create such ambiguity. In doing so, we begin to appreciate some of the limits of our own perceptions that we have been ignoring.

Unexpected information can be intriguing. For instance, words often suggest a certain meaning that doesn't describe the reality. For example, most of us assume that anything "natural" is also "healthy." Imagine my shock when a noted cancer researcher told me that alfalfa sprouts, to me the very epitome of natural and healthy, are carcinogenic. You practically had to pick me off the floor when she next told me that "artificial" ingredients in some foods, such as the preservatives in bread, were anti-carcinogens, materials that help to prevent cancer.

Having an experience that disproves a long-held belief can also be very good for developing interest in finding out what else might not be true. I often encounter people who automatically equate doing more with accomplishing more. For instance, a student was preparing for a graduate-school entrance examination. In her thinking, the more practice tests she took, the better her eventual score would be. By the time I met her, she had already completed almost all prior tests and practice tests provided by different publishers. While she certainly improved by engaging in this approach, she also unintentionally developed powerful habits for making errors in some circumstances. When she came to me, I was easily able to diagnose her mistaken habits. However, because she had taken so many practice tests, it was quite challenging to develop a way for her to eliminate the habits and replace them with better ways of answering questions. When the method I outlined required less than 1 percent of the time that she had used to develop the bad habits, she was fascinated to realize how efficient it is to just practice the right things in the right way, rather than practice the most things in any possible way.

If you encounter someone who has had a spiritual experience you've always wondered about, hearing and asking questions about the experience can also be quite intriguing. I observe this all the time relative to my descriptions of having been quickly healed after prayer and receiving dictations of words to include in my books. An investigation center could build on such interest by offering classes or events where spiritual experiences would be described and discussed, along with the Biblical background for understanding more about what had happened.

Possibilities can also be intriguing. A large number of people are fascinated by the potential of various kinds of technology, whether to cure diseases, to visit other planets, or to construct microscopic machines to work with amazing effectiveness in difficult environments. Having people knowledgeable about such subjects interpret current knowledge and how it is and can be applied would attract many people who might not come to a center for discussions of faith or spirituality.

High achievers often study ways to improve. If a center offers courses taught by those with great expertise and reputation in self-improvement, undoubtedly many people who would like to be the best would be eager to learn while taking such courses.

I'm sure by now you have your own ideas about how to add intriguing elements to an investigation center. Let's now turn to credibility in the next lesson.

Lesson Thirteen Assignments

1. How has something being intriguing assisted people you know to try something new and learn valuable lessons?

2. How could investigation centers become intriguing in ways that would greatly increase how many people learn?

3. What other ways of being intriguing do you think could attract more learners?

4. How might investigation centers be improved by becoming intriguing in ways that are seldom available?

5. How has something being intriguing enabled you to learn and accomplish more than you otherwise would have?

6. Which of the ways of being intriguing that helped you to learn and achieve more should be provided to others?

Lesson Fourteen:

Credible

Finally, brethren, whatever things are true,
whatever things are noble, whatever things are just,
whatever things are pure, whatever things are lovely,
whatever things are of good report,
if there is any virtue and
if there is anything praiseworthy —
meditate on these things.

— Philippians 4:8 (NKJV)

"Credible" is another word missing from most Bible translations. Despite this, being credible is as important as is being truthful for attracting people to and helping them learn from an investigation center. Here's why: When the truth doesn't sound accurate to hearers, people will treat the truth as through it were not true ... potentially even believing in and acting on an untruth, something that could even be a lie from the enemy who is in the world.

Establishing credibility for unexpected, new information can be difficult. Hearers may lack the relevant skills, knowledge, and experience to appreciate even well-documented facts. If the information is also at odds with what a reader or hearer has long "known" to be true, establishing credibility can be even more difficult.

Here's an example. As a teenager, I discovered that a friend's mother was diabetic. I didn't know what that term meant, so I asked some questions. The mother told me about testing her blood sugar, taking insulin, and then drinking a big glass of orange juice to "counteract" the insulin. As a simple-minded newcomer to the information, I couldn't understand why someone would consume a lot of sugar after just taking insulin to reduce blood sugar. Such an action seemed self-defeating to me, and I said so. The mother screwed up her face in puzzlement over how to respond to my observation. After a moment, she said that the doctors had told her to do so and they must be right. As you may not know, the practice of drinking orange juice in connection with insulin injections was later discovered to be harmful to diabetics. Simple logic on this point prior to that time of discovery, however, wasn't credible when coming from a teenage boy trying to apply common sense to the facts.

Lest we feel superior while considering that example, I'm sure we are all conditioned to do things that make no sense, simply because someone respected once told us to do so. In my own case, I have a hard time not changing the oil in my car every 3,000 miles, even though my car's electronic display tells me that my oil still has a lot of life left in it. I still feel a need to follow the advice that my father and able mechanics gave me while growing up: Engine oil should be changed every 3,000 miles.

What are some of the ways that credibility can be established? A demonstration can be ideal. Tell someone what should happen as a result and then make it happen. Before you get too excited about such an approach, realize that magicians do so all of the time to trick people. Since the audience has agreed in advance to be fooled in exchange for being entertained, there's no harm done. However, be sure that your demonstrations don't contain any tricks. Ideally, have your demonstrations be ones that a visitor to the center can do for herself or himself with a minimum of preparations. By doing so, you will not only increase credibility, you will also enable visitors to share what they learn in credible ways with others, thus multiplying the fruitfulness of the investigation center.

Many times logic alone is used to establish credibility, but you have to be careful with logic. Words express assumptions, cultural perspectives, and historical associations that can color an argument to make it appear to be true while it is actually false. For instance, listen to the opening arguments to the jury by the prosecutor and the defendant's lawyer in a criminal case, and you often won't be able to tell who is closer to being right. Also, the enemy who is in the world is highly skilled at twisting words just a bit to tweak us into doing something that opposes God.

For believers, checking what the Bible says should be an essential part of testing any new information or knowledge. In doing so, be sure to reflect on what the whole Bible says, rather than just relying on a short phrase from one verse.

Unfortunately, nonbelievers will often see the Bible as a suspect source of credibility. As in a court, witnesses can be important for adding credibility. If someone respectable can describe an occurrence and answer questions about it, some will take what is said more seriously. However, if the witness can also provide objective information that can be independently checked, then the credibility of the witness's testimony will be substantially bolstered, such as happens with an expert. When objective information isn't available, it may be possible to find other reliable witnesses who can verify what the first witness said. While not as good as providing timeless, objective proof, such bolstering by a number of witnesses is better than doing nothing to help people appreciate the truth.

Be careful that the supplied credibility adequately supports what is being advocated. I often see people of faith not being sufficiently careful in doing so. For instance, someone who has been miraculously healed following prayer might regard that experience as sufficient evidence that his or her faith is valid. While that experience is adequate to convince the healed person, it may not make much of an impression on someone else. For instance, there are probably people who have been miraculously healed in similar ways who belong to other faiths. Unless the evidence is unique (such as Jesus instantly healing lepers, something that is not described elsewhere as having been done by anyone else at the time) and verifiable (such as by "before" and "after" photographs that reveal to experts no indication of having been altered) in a variety of credible ways, such evidence won't establish the bigger point. Instead, the evidence will only support the conclusion that something miraculous once happened to a person of a certain faith in the practice of such beliefs.

Appreciate that almost all documentation could be attacked in ways that will create doubt, whether such attacks are justified or not. For example, someone can simply make an unfounded charge about the documentation having been altered. Most people will lose interest in hearing a truthful answer about the documentation not having been altered, long before the answer has been developed and related. In such circumstances, some people will just assume that alteration is likely. When such inaccurate views develop, introducing documentation may have had the effect of reducing, rather than increasing, credibility.

Rather than simply supplying a single basis for the credibility of what is asserted, I suggest that investigation centers be prepared to provide a variety of credible evidence. When such preparations have been done in advance, visitors can then be asked what forms of credibility would be most helpful. Should people greatly differ in their responses, a leader should adjust the activity, class, course, event, experience, or program in a way that would permit each person to focus on whatever evidence would be most meaningful to her or him. Doing so might require splitting the group at least temporarily. Or, in cases where the variety of desired credible proof requested is predictably the greatest, the activity or program could always be conducted one-on-one.

I often find that people take a too academic approach while adding credibility. People who are not academics (nor wish to be) can find academic evidence to be irrelevant and uninteresting. That's one reason why demonstrations can be so effective. While a demonstration can be excellent for exploring something involving the physical world, I'm sure you realize that many spiritual truths are difficult to demonstrate in similarly striking ways. Consider that providing opportunities for spiritual experiences can help someone to appreciate such a truth. For instance, a guided, silent retreat is surely going to help someone awaken spiritually to realizing that his or her true self is actually different from part of the way that she or he conducts his or her life. Consequently, I advocate direct experience as being the best way to make information or knowledge more credible. When every part of yourself (both physically and spiritually) has been engaged with something, you know the truth (or lack thereof) in a complete way that cannot be otherwise duplicated.

Many people will object to my advocacy of direct experience by observing that some things cannot be experienced. For instance, I cannot become one legged without having one leg removed. I totally accept that point. However, almost anything can be experienced in a simulated way that will convey some important aspects of such circumstances. For instance, the idea of dyslexia (mixing up letters in words and sentences) was abstract and unclear to me until someone asked me to read a page adjusted to appear as it might to someone with dyslexia. I was immediately filled with comprehension that I do not think I could have gained in less experiential ways. I also gained insights into how to help such individuals that would never have occurred to me prior to the experience.

Let us again consider experiencing being one-legged. I am sure there's a way to bind one of my legs so I couldn't use it for any normal purpose, such as by tying my foot to the back of my thigh. While my balance wouldn't be the same as after actually losing a leg, perhaps that change could also be simulated by adding weights to my "remaining" leg. As I tried to get around and do my normal activities, I am sure I would acquire some understanding of what it means to have one leg. I certainly wouldn't gain all of the desirable understanding, but I would surely gain some useful knowledge from the experience.

Providing people with experiences is much more time consuming, a great deal more expensive, and requires much more work for those who plan and organize activities, classes, courses, events, and programs. Planners and organizers often have limited time, patience, experience, and attention to devote to such tasks. Here's where conducting global contests can be a huge benefit by attracting many more people to participate in improving ideas for how to do so.

As I've written in other books, the current best thinking about contests for developing better practices is to first be quite narrow in what is considered. Thus, if you could either look at how to conduct better simulations in general or just better simulations of being one-legged, the latter approach would work much better. Next, you need to relate the outcomes being sought. For instance, in the one-legged simulation, your outcome might be for a higher percentage of those having the experience to more appropriately help one-legged people. Another desired outcome might be for the total cost of the simulation to be substantially reduced from the current level and require relatively little time of the participants. After identifying such desired outcomes, you should make as many people as possible aware of the contest.

The contest rules can help. For example, offer prizes and recognition. Additionally, any entrant should be allowed to propose improvements to any other submission. That's because many people can contribute by making small changes that are beneficial, while few can ascertain sizable improvements. When such contests have been conducted in this way, the results have usually been much better than if submissions could not be partially duplicated. Ultimately, people who conduct these contests should encourage experimentation and publication of the results so that everyone can learn from applying what appears to be useful. If you would like to know more about how such contests might be best conducted, the nonprofit edition of *Excellent Solutions* (400 Year Project Press, 2014) by me is a good source. For a less detailed treatment of the subject, see *The Ul-*

timate Competitive Advantage (Berrett-Koehler, 2003), authored by Carol Coles and me.

We next explore how being involved with investigation centers can be rewarding for visitors in Lesson Fifteen.

Lesson Fourteen Assignments

1. How has something being credible assisted people you know to try something new and learn valuable lessons?

2. How could investigation centers become credible in ways that would greatly increase how many people learn?

3. What other ways of being credible do you think could attract more learners?

4. How might investigation centers be improved by becoming more credible in ways that are seldom available?

5. How has something being credible enabled you to learn and accomplish more than you otherwise would have?

6. Which of the ways of being credible that helped you to learn and achieve more should be provided to others?

Lesson Fifteen:

Rewarding

"For what profit is it to a man
if he gains the whole world, and loses his own soul?
Or what will a man give in exchange for his soul?
For the Son of Man will come
in the glory of His Father with His angels, and
then He will reward each according to his works."

— Matthew 16:26-27 (NKJV)

Unlike some of the words we've considered that describe desirable qualities of an investigation center, "rewarding" and "rewards" can be found in Bible translations. These words show up positively and negatively, as well as ironically. Clearly, God has given considerable thought to rewarding us and to what rewards to provide.

Let's start by considering Salvation. Of course, Salvation is not something that we earn. It's a gift we receive from God after having believed in Jesus and accepting Him as Lord and Savior, because of His precious sacrifice and resurrection from the dead to overcome sin and death for all time.

While Salvation is not a reward, accepting this most wonderful gift can certainly feel rewarding. Consequently, for those who are not yet believers, Salvation can be mistakenly viewed as being a reward for coming to an investigation center. Such a perception can confuse someone spiritually. Watch out in this regard, so you can correct any misunderstandings!

The most important point is to never lose sight of opportunities to help people understand what it means to believe in and follow Jesus as Lord and Savior. In doing so, we should be careful to avoid presenting the Gospel in such a way that someone will be confused or choose to run from, rather than to, accepting Salvation.

While parts of the Bible describe Jesus allocating rewards in accordance with the works each person has done, most of such references are not specific about what are the rewards. Parables describing good stewards of His resources (such as the ones involving minas and talents) suggest that part of such rewards could be to gain increased responsibilities. Since we will reign with Jesus upon His return, these parables could be alluding to ongoing tasks for faithful servants in this regard throughout eternity.

However, Jesus did specifically reveal aspects of what is required to obtain such rewards. For instance, Jesus said that some potential rewards will be withheld from the people who gained recognition while alive for works that had been done. In order to gain Godly rewards from Jesus, we are encouraged to perform works for Him privately and secretly. Our purpose should solely be to increase and improve His Kingdom by doing His will in ways that glorify Him. Then, He will consider us to be good and faithful servants.

While it is all well and good to stay focused on eternity in whatever we do, we need to remember that visitors to investigation centers may initially be much more short-term in their interests. We should be sure to respond to whatever interests them or seems most pressing.

Rather than assume what rewards to provide, it's best to ask what the visitor prefers, just as we should do concerning credible evidence. After receiving whatever reward is sought, visitors are more likely to then seek rewards they had not previously considered.

Let's review the unmet needs discussed in Part One, so we can imagine some of the rewards that visitors might seek. In preparing what is done by an investigation center, we should be able to help someone receive any of such rewards.

We will begin with misunderstandings. Because of having misunderstood something, people may have suffered roadblocks to accomplishing important results or experienced damage to significant relationships. Eliminating, diminishing, or avoiding these roadblocks and damage will seem quite rewarding to those who feel stymied or are stalled, especially after the first improvement occurs.

By obtaining answers to questions they have long been mulling, visitors may gain peace about what has been troubling them, be able to accomplish more in terms of what is difficult, or gain understanding that opens doors to perceiving and grasping new opportunities.

In satisfying curiosity, the pleasures of learning may be experienced, along with enjoying greater confidence while engaging in related activities. In addition, further curiosity could be stimulated, permitting other enjoyable information searches and discoveries.

After overcoming discomfort, some visitors may gain a feeling of peace that's greater than what has been experienced by them in some time. The quality of their day-to-day lives may also improve. Further, hope may be increased in ways that encourage engaging in more fruitful activities for God's Kingdom.

People who gain friendly fellowship may benefit by experiencing more joy, doing more pleasant activities with a companion or friend, and feeling pleased while sharing their most important experiences.

Naturally, those whose hurts have been healed will feel as if they have been greatly rewarded. The pain that was once the center of their existence will gradually dull and fade away. While many visitors will not realize the price that they have been paying for various hang-ups vainly used to avoid more pain, putting those hang-ups behind them will free up much time that can be devoted to more useful and satisfying pursuits.

For someone who has been spiritually dead, a single spiritual experience could feel like discovering the best part of life. With more of such experiences, a new or a deeper relationship with God can be developed. Since God can provide the most satisfying ways of living, a spiritual experience with Him allows someone to obtain whatever would be most rewarding. One such reward could be developing a sense of gratitude for what God has provided. Life, what is in the world around us, the people we know, and how our needs are met can all seem miraculous when we but take a moment to contemplate them in peaceful silence and rest.

How might the availability of such rewards best be conveyed? I believe that video testimonials, as well as stories related by investigation-center volunteers and staff, could greatly help. I know that I have been drawn to engage in some richly rewarding programs only after hearing someone talk about what the experience has been like in terms of the benefits that he or she had gained.

In addition, an investigation center should encourage the visitors who have gained any desired rewards to share their experiences and related feelings with family, friends, coworkers, and neighbors. In the process of encouraging such sharing, I strongly urge investigation centers to inquire about what aspects of visitors' experiences have been good, neutral, unpleasant, and harmful. In terms of what has been good, ask what rewards someone feels that she or he has gained. In doing so, you may identify other rewards that many other people would like to obtain, as well.

So far in this lesson, we have focused on visitors. However, we should not forget that an investigation center should also be rewarding for volunteers and staff. Many organizations forget to consider such people and proceed to design and maintain roles for them that are quite undesirable. Believe me when I say that if the staff and volunteers find being involved with investigation centers to be unrewarding, so will many visitors ... due to bearing the brunt of dissatisfaction strongly felt by those providing the services.

Especially for some young people (whose presence as staff and volunteers can make an investigation center more appealing to many visitors), "making a difference" will be very often seen as a desirable reward. While each individual will describe what difference-making

114

means in various ways, one key element will be seeing positive results from taking an action. For someone answering questions about what the investigation center does, one such difference could be as simple as a visitor deciding to engage in something the center offers. If the visitor later gains some important benefit, the question answerer can feel rewarded by finding out about that result. Be sure to set up information systems that enable volunteers and staff to follow how their efforts have had any impact on visitors and others at the center.

Some staff and volunteers will be involved at a center because of an experience connected to a Godly calling for assisting others who have had similar experiences. While much of what volunteers and staff do will provide direct impressions of how effective they are, it's also valuable to ask those they interact with to give feedback designed to help staff and volunteers become even more effective. Otherwise, it can seem to a staff member or volunteer as if no one but God cares about what he or she is doing. Being in such a situation can feel unrewarding, the opposite of what an investigation center should seek to accomplish.

An investigation center will also have an impact on people other than visitors, volunteers, and staff, such as neighbors. A great way to benefit neighbors is by providing special events that make them feel appreciated.

Vendors to the center, such as landlords, suppliers, and lessors of equipment, should also see their connections to the center as being rewarding. Otherwise, difficulties will arise that could harm the center's ability to expand and improve God's Kingdom.

While I continue for now to avoid the subject of paying for the costs of a center, I'm sure you agree that at least some centers will encourage donations of money, goods, and services. While in countries such as the United States donors may receive some practical benefit in the form of tax deductions, such a reward will be inadequate to stimulate many donations. Some potential donors will also be interested in receiving recognition on Earth, rather than solely waiting for the heavenly rewards mentioned in the Bible. Ways of providing such recognition will be important in those cases, especially for nonbelievers.

Ask current and potential donors what they would most like to know and then provide it to them. Otherwise, your investigation center will be much less rewarding than it could be, especially if delivery of services to visitors will be affected by how much is donated.

Even for those who primarily want Earthly recognition, many will also have an interest in understanding the center's effects on visitors, especially in the form of objective information and descriptions shared by those who have benefitted from their involvement. Of course, those who are seeking nothing more than expanding and improving God's Kingdom will also want to be informed about the results in doing so. Providing such relevant information can be quite valuable for helping donors feel rewarded for their involvement.

There's one final group that I would like to suggest you reward: those who initially set up an investigation center. While the Holy Spirit will, no doubt, have provided an empowering vision of what God wants to be accomplished and a sense of how doing so will please God, such founders often regard what follows with as much interest as a parent does about her or his first offspring. In fact, some founders may be individuals who have not been blessed with the opportunity to be parents, and the center will be somewhat like a surrogate for a biological child.

If I have missed anyone who should be rewarded, please let me know. I look forward to receiving e-mails from you. Please share your observations by e-mail to donmitchell@fastforward400.com/.

We turn now to Part Three, where we consider possible models for investigation centers.

Lesson Fifteen Assignments

1. How has being rewarded assisted people you know to try something new and learn valuable lessons?

2. How could investigation centers become rewarding in ways that would greatly increase how many people learn?

3. What other ways of being rewarding do you think could attract more learners?

4. How might investigation centers be improved by becoming more rewarding to visitors in ways that are seldom available?

5. How has something being rewarding enabled you to learn and accomplish more than you otherwise would?

6. Which of the ways of being rewarding that helped you to learn and achieve more should be provided to others?

7. How should the center reward volunteers, staff, neighbors, suppliers, donors, founders, and other stakeholders?

Part Three:

Possible Models

*Jesus said to him, "I am the way, the truth, and the life.
No one comes to the Father except through Me."*

— John 14:6 (NKJV)

In Part One, *Investigation Centers* outlines seven unmet needs that could be served. In Part Two, we consider eight qualities that would make an investigation center more fruitful in expanding and improving God's Kingdom in serving those unmet needs. Now, in Part Three, we turn to eight possible models for supplying these qualities. In each lesson, we consider one model to stimulate thinking about what to do at an investigation center. In supplying the eight qualities, we should always keep in mind that Jesus is our ultimate model for anything that should be accomplished, our perfect source of how to proceed, of truth, and of the right way to live.

We begin in Lesson Sixteen by looking at various ways that organizations, activities, and people have established themselves near to those they serve. We consider possible implications for what an investigation center might do to accomplish even more. Drawing on Jesus' perspective, we should keep in mind the way that filling each believer with the Holy Spirit establishes nearness to God by actually being inside someone, gradually transforming each one.

Many people today feel adrift, isolated, and ignored. Some of the pain of these feelings can be assuaged by being in an environment where it's considered proper to just hang out, even alone, doing little or nothing. Increasingly, coffee bars play this role. We consider how to make an investigation center feel like a comfortable, informal hangout in Lesson Seventeen.

In almost every nation, the standard for increasing enjoyment of any activity is to make it more entertaining. It's as if nothing can be satisfying unless the experience is lively and intriguing enough. While their youngsters climb elaborate gyms and race around mazes, some indoor playgrounds offer entertainment and snacks for parents. Lesson Eighteen focuses on making investigation centers entertaining.

Many people today prefer to take charge of what's intended. Doing so allows them more independence, flexibility, and comfort. Letting people do things on their own is also a great way to serve more people at less cost. Done properly, the experience can feel superior to even great, all-inclusive service for meeting certain needs. In Lesson Nineteen, we explore what aspects of visitors doing things for themselves should be available at investigation centers.

Even people who normally don't indulge in overeating can find it hard to ignore having dozens of their favorite foods presented in high quality, unlimited quantity at a fixed price. The preceding sentence is a way of describing a restaurant or function that offers ample buffets. While buffets are often more expensive than a normal meal, the value often seems relatively greater. In Lesson Twenty, we investigate how an investigation center's offerings can feel like grazing at an unending, delightful buffet, but without the drawback of gaining weight!

I don't like to go to movie theaters, in part because their floors always seem to be sticky from patrons who have spilled candy and beverages. However, when it comes to the Internet, site owners seek to make what visitors experience so compelling that people remain longer than they intend, do more there than they plan, and return more frequently than would otherwise make any sense. Doing so is called "stickiness," an attribute that operates almost like a powerful elastic band to keep someone connected. We'll explore applying this concept in Lesson Twenty-One.

When I buy my wife a piece of jewelry, the first question she asks is, "It is real or costume?" Since she doesn't want me to spend money on jewelry with genuine jewels and pearls, she sighs with relief when I tell her that the piece is costume. However, when it comes to something important in other areas of life, she wants the genuine article. For instance, she doesn't want me to pretend to love her. She wants me to truly love her. We consider many of the aspects of genuineness that can make an investigation center more appealing in Lesson Twenty-Two.

Rest and sleep are important parts of being able to function during the demanding and active parts of our days. However, even if we allow much time for rest and sleep, we won't get much benefit from such time commitments unless we experience enough peace so that we can empty our conscious minds. When we remove harmful mental and physical distractions from the rest of the days, our lives are better, as well. We investigate ways an investigation center can contribute to peacefulness in Lesson-Twenty-Three.

We turn now to Lesson Sixteen: Near.

Lesson Sixteen:

Near

The Lord is near to all who call upon Him,
To all who call upon Him in truth.

— Psalm 145:18 (NKJV)

As Part Three's introduction notes, God is near to us in many ways. First, believers are filled with the Holy Spirit, eliminating any separation between God and them. By praying in the name of Jesus, believers can speak directly to our Heavenly Father. The Holy Spirit brings knowledge, wisdom, power, and direction to transform the believer into being more like Jesus. Second, as Psalm 145:18 (NKJV) observes, when we call on the Lord in truth, He is near. Third, Matthew 18:20 (NKJV) tells us that whenever two or more people are gathered together in the name of Jesus, He is present with them.

Contrast these Godly presences with what a nonbeliever perceives and experiences. While the Holy Spirit stirs nonbelievers' interest in being connected to God, the Holy Spirit will not be inside and improving such a person. In addition, nonbelievers are rarely going to be calling on God in truth, meaning that they will not perceive Him as being near ... because He isn't for them. While nonbelievers may be present at times when Jesus is there with believers, it is usually hard to notice what you don't believe in. Even if you do notice aspects of His presence that exceed your belief, you might develop an alternate explanation. For instance, nonbelievers I know often provide me with their own "scientific" explanations for the twelve times that God has miraculously healed me. As they do, it's clear to me that they don't feel comfortable with the idea that I might have experienced these miracles. I also sense that some of them want to "one-up" me, as a way they can feel superior.

When I think about these differences between nonbelievers and believers in terms of being and perceiving to be near God, I often wonder how anyone ever comes to the point of choosing to be saved. As a result, I'm not surprised by how often people tell me that they made the Salvation decision while or just after experiencing a severe life crisis, major illness, or painful setback. When our desires aren't happening and our needs are great, we are more likely to seek Him.

Keeping these differences in spiritual nearness to God in mind, let's now consider how nearness affects us in day-to-day, secular living. As Lesson Eight discusses, nearness can save us time, a form of convenience that almost everyone values. I often see this characteristic helping a doughnut-shop chain that operates near where I live. While not everyone is looking for a daily doughnut, many people like to have a cup of coffee or tea to sip while driving or riding, especially when tired and needing a little pick-me-up.

When I first came to the Boston area, this chain typically had one store per town and several in the major cities. The usual distance from home or work to a store was about three miles. Since then, the chain has opened as many shops as possible, while also adding small operations in many gas stations. Consequently, it's hard to travel more than one mile now, except in the towns that successfully resist such outlets, without passing at least one shop. In high traffic areas, such places are located even closer together. I was reminded of that fact when my wife asked me where a bank branch was. I told her it was next to such a store on a given street. She immediately said she knew where that store was. A few seconds later I remembered that there are two such stores on that street. She might not have found what she was looking for if I hadn't clarified the location of the store near the branch.

Such nearness has several effects. First, it makes me much more aware of possibly stopping for a beverage or some food. Second, each time I pass a location during a drive or walk, my resistance to stopping and purchasing decreases. Third, I am eventually reminded that the chain gives me rewards for buying. Right now, I have an incentive to visit five times as soon as possible ... doing so will double the frequency of my receiving "free" beverages. While I already have six unused coupons for "free" beverages, it's hard for me to resist the allure of receiving yet another one. Fourth, if I am pressed for time to eat lunch or dinner, I'll think about briefly stopping to pick up one of the chain's quickly prepared chicken-salad sandwiches.

For nearness to cause visiting, my most important needs must match what the doughnut-store chain offers. Otherwise, I wouldn't stop, any more than I would stop at a store that only sells hand guns and ammunition while on my way to church. So when the doughnut-store chain added sandwiches, it greatly expanded the relevance of its nearness for me ... especially when I'm hungry and pressed for time in the afternoon or evening.

An investigation center could go the doughnut-store chain one better in terms of relevance by serving a broader variety of immediate needs ... possibly including great beverages, doughnuts, snacks, and sandwiches. The investigation center could even choose to be, in part, an outlet for the chain. Or investigation centers could even establish their own chain.

A local credit union had an idea for connecting to such an outlet. For a branch located in a strip mall, the credit union lobby, while open, connects directly into the doughnut-store chain. While in the credit union, you smell the coffee and doughnuts. As a result, many people leave the credit union via the doughnut shop to make a purchase there. I've also noticed quite a few people enter the credit union from the doughnut store after having had a snack. Unlike nearby banks that offer only stale, lukewarm coffee to customers, this credit union's customers enjoy better and fresher coffee and food, ones that cost the credit union nothing. Thus, the credit union has come closer to its customers in a more relevant way that helps both businesses do better.

This example makes me think of a food court at a large shopping mall. By having so many choices, many shoppers head there with family and friends, allowing each person to scurry off to purchase food from a different specialty vendor. One child might have a slice of cheese pizza, while another one eats a healthy chicken salad, mom has a delicious smoothie, and dad chows down on a hefty, roast-beef sandwich.

Done correctly, an investigation center might find a way to cluster with many complementary activities in the same vicinity to increase visits for one and all. In fact, such a center could even be located in a shopping mall, perhaps adjacent to the food court. The center might offer choices that would enable the whole family to find something individually engaging to do there, especially while wanting a respite from busy shopping or other chores. The potential of doing so is underscored by the success of the entertainment venues that are increasingly being included in larger malls, such as the amusement rides at Minnesota's Mall of America.

Other places that people regularly visit could provide similar opportunities for joint attraction. For instance, supermarkets are increasingly including other kinds of outlets, such as bank branches, prescription pharmacies, and take-out food counters. Some supermarket chains might be open to making a section of their parking lots available for installing investigation centers, especially if the activities occurring there would increase how often people visit the supermarkets.

Schools are another place where families often go. While due to legal restrictions public schools aren't usually going to permit an investigation center inside, in many cases there are locations that could be opened within sight and walking distance for before- and after-school and related activities to be attended by the students and their families. Christian schools might well provide some space inside for the same purposes.

While I could go on to point out other locations where people often go, I'm sure you've thought of one: work. Most people spend more hours at their work locations than at any other place away from home. If investigation centers could be near to such work, many people would find it more attractive to participate before and after work, as well as during meal breaks.

Notice that as investigation centers are located in more places, common branding and signage could increase the sensitivity to their presence for those in the areas, including occasional passers-by, to opportunities being present that fit the observer's needs. Thus, as investigation centers proliferate around various places where many people go, awareness of a given center will also increase.

Of course, many people spend more time while awake online, as well as talking and texting on their cell phones, than they do at anything other than work. Naturally, if investigation centers can provide online and cell-phone experiences that are more engaging than the alternatives, then the centers' offerings will be present at almost all times for virtually everyone in the advanced economies. While any inappropriate content that attracts people to some online sites should not be duplicated by an investigation center, it's increasingly clear that much of what is seen via electronic connections is of more value to providers of content or owners of such connections than to visitors. Even many nonprofit sites are susceptible to being harmed by those who are determined to gain unfair economic advantages. As a result, some sincere people could develop a desire to access more reliable sources of information. Investigation centers might, as a result, gain an advantage in credibility that's second to none, due to just being careful about what information is shared.

Just when you thought that I had run out of ways to be nearer, let me suggest another opportunity: radio broadcasting. Many people listen to radio stations while driving, especially for long distances. Such occasions can be excellent for offering extended programming that delves into the kinds of subjects that everyone is curious about, but that are seldom covered on television or radio. To make such programming available, commercial time could be bought on popular radio stations and networks. If substantial funds are available, stations could even be purchased and their programming shifted to this purpose.

Naturally, television can also be an opportunity. One low-cost option is to provide programming that offers a taste of what can be experienced at an investigation center via cable services. Production costs can be cut by using the free resources at local-access broadcasting studios.

Now, I'm sure you are convinced that there's nothing else that can be done. However, if you think that, you are mistaken. There's no reason why there need only be one kind of investigation center. Why not have different types of investigation centers that narrowly focus on certain kinds of people? For instance, for older people, senior centers tend to cater to those with lower incomes. Some older individuals might enjoy visiting investigation centers that focus on their needs regardless of their financial situations. Younger people, of course, usually want to congregate only with others their own age. When that's not possible in one place, some younger people go elsewhere. Similarly, parents of young children have a lot to say to one another, and some may be looking for compatible play dates with well-behaved children.

In the same way that some people swear by the coffee at one outlet, while others wouldn't touch it with a ten-foot pole, I suspect that there's an important opportunity to add nearness by similar investigation centers competing with one another for similar kinds of visitors. You might be thinking that doing so would be financial idiocy. However, think back to the early church. After being banished from the synagogues, many believers met in their homes. By making use of homes once again, nearness could be extended into literally every neighborhood with believers in it, the places where people spend most of their early mornings, evenings, and nights. By drawing on the goodwill of people who want to advance and improve God's Kingdom by serving in this way, investigation centers could become more than near. They could become ubiquitous.

Lest we become complacent about how best to increase nearness, we should always be asking potential visitors to investigation centers where else they would like to have opportunities for such engagement. For instance, many people like to have some content included during their trips and vacations. Tour organizers could provide investigation-center-type learning as well as program-related experiences. Those who have never been on a spiritual retreat could have the opportunity to participate in a long weekend centered on such engagement. And, of course, there's no reason why there couldn't be investigation centers operating with relevant programming on cruise ships, at resorts, within spas, and in corners of museums. Since the added appeal might bring in more visitors to such locales, investigation centers might find a warm welcome from some of such enterprises.

As I am sure you can see by now, ubiquity can eventually be turned into being almost unavoidable, especially if investigation centers provide desired programming that isn't otherwise available.

We look next, in Lesson Seventeen, at investigation centers serving as hangouts.

Lesson Sixteen Assignments

1. How has being near to a source of learning helped people you know to try something new and absorb valuable lessons?

2. How could investigation centers become nearer in ways that would greatly increase how many people learn?

3. What other ways of being near could attract more learners?

4. How might investigation centers be improved by becoming nearer to visitors in ways that are seldom available?

5. How has something being near enabled you to learn and accomplish more than you otherwise would?

6. Which of the ways of being near that helped you to learn and achieve more should be provided to others?

7. How should the center use nearness to attract and retain the support of more volunteers, staff, neighbors, suppliers, donors, founders, and other stakeholders?

Lesson Seventeen:

Hang Out

Unless the Lord builds the house,
They labor in vain who build it;
Unless the Lord guards the city,
The watchman stays awake in vain.

— Psalm 127:1 (NKJV)

While nearness will increase the likelihood that people will visit an investigation center, how long visitors stay during the first occasion and how often they return depend on the appeal experienced while there. When I think of a place being appealing, I associate that concept, in part, with being somewhere I like to hang out for extended periods of time, either with other people or by myself, one of the ways I enjoy being with God.

I was reminded just the other day of how nearness and appeal combine. On my way to a meeting, I drove down a street I had not traveled on for many years. Along the way, I passed an aboveground water reservoir in our town, a place where my wife and I often had pleasant picnics when our company offices were located nearby. I immediately thought that she and I should start doing so again on warm days when we are both in town. So, here is a case where nearness and desirability for hanging out will probably combine to cause some pleasant time to be spent together at an appealing spot.

I next ruminated about places where I like to hang out when the weather isn't so good. Our town's library is one of those places. As an avid reader who frequently borrows and returns volumes, I have gotten to know almost everyone on the staff. I'm also likely to run into people I know there. Pleasant conversations always follow. After picking up books on cold winter days, I like to retire to a comfortable room there where the furnishings are more reminiscent of an oversized living room than of a library's study area. I prefer the northeast corner in that room, a spot filled with natural and artificial light. The chair is just the right size for me to curl up in. I often spend the whole Sunday afternoon there after church, happily enjoying my reading.

Sometimes, I do something else at the library on Sunday afternoons: Attend a free concert. Professional musicians like to rehearse with a live audience before performing a paid gig. The library's music committee is filled with knowledgeable people who are well connected to local musicians who seek such rehearsal opportunities. The performers the committee picks have often won international prizes. As a result, the quality of performances is always superior. Before the concerts, I enjoy chatting about the program with committee members and those seated around me. During the performances, I love watching the children who attend, seeing them drink in the music's beauty. There's a reception afterward, and I have plenty of opportunities then to speak to the musicians. In the process, I always feel that I've made interesting connections and been blessed with a fine Sabbath experience, enjoying part of the goodness that God so generously provides.

Thinking about those Sunday afternoon performances reminds me that many local organizations offer either free or reduced-price concerts of all kinds on other days. While attending such events, I similarly get to know the staffers who work at the venues, see other "regulars" whose taste in music is similar to mine, and meet other audience members during intermissions and occasional receptions. On rare occasions, I'm invited to performances and receptions primarily attended by professional musicians I admire, and I enjoy getting to know these performers as individuals in a less "on-stage" environment. The musicians, in turn, seem to enjoy meeting some fans during a relaxing time for them.

On my way to and from such events, I often have spare time. Naturally, I look for a hangout. The most comfortable one usually turns out to be a Starbucks outlet that mostly attracts college students. In many ways, this hangout serves my needs similarly to the comfortable room at the library, except that I can also sip a hot or iced beverage. I carry a library book with me on such occasions and read enjoyably ... unless I happen to be seated near a noisy clack of students trying to impress one another. However, most of the students are usually busy on their computers, working away in almost total silence, completely engrossed.

Let me now consider the other side of hanging out. Where don't I hang out? Well, there are many places where I would like to hang out, but I don't. For instance, less than a block away from the Starbucks outlet I frequent, there is an independent coffee shop that is more spacious and attractive. However, while there I feel a need to leave immediately after finishing a beverage. Also, almost everyone in the independent coffee shop is having a conversation. If I wanted to have coffee with a friend, I would go here instead of Starbucks. However, we wouldn't really hang out. We would just meet there for a beverage or snack, have a brief chat, and leave.

Many food outlets affect me in the same "move-on" manner. Some even have signs that suggest no "loitering." A similar impression can be conveyed by how the seating is arranged. The doughnut-shop chain I spoke about in Lesson Sixteen has a store located between the two coffee-bar outlets I've just described. However, the doughnut-shop store has almost no seats. The tables there are usually quite dirty, which makes them unappealing. In addition, the seats and tables are located near the door, which opens directly to the outdoors. If it's cold, hot, or windy outside, you receive an unwelcome reminder of those unpleasant conditions every time the door opens or closes. In addition, the din of nearby traffic greatly increases at such times. The subliminal message I receive is: Drink and eat quickly, then move on.

If you want to eat or drink during a performance, many places resist your doing so. Due to wanting to avoid spills, clean-up costs, and attracting pests, many theaters and concert halls won't let you carry anything with you to a seat other than bottled water. Countering that standard, many Boston-area theatrical venues now encourage eating and drinking during performances. While doing so certainly contributes to making a mess, I'm sure that some of those who are marginally interested in a performance find the occasions more bearable if they can also snack and drink with family and friends. The venues also profit by attracting more customers, and making more food and beverage sales.

Another way that food and beverage outlets convey a willingness to be a hangout is by providing free WiFi. With such access, almost any outlet will attract at least some people working for hours at a time on laptops or tablet computers.

How service is provided can also serve to make a place more of a hangout. There are a number of restaurants near the free and reduced-price concerts that serve alcoholic beverages. Some of these places have television sets located almost everywhere, seeming to invite visitors to watch whatever programs they like for extended time periods. If the staff also discreetly leaves you alone, you can enjoy hanging out in such a location, especially if you want to watch a sporting event with others. By choosing to sit either with others or by yourself, you can determine how much social interaction you will have. Unless there are no empty seats and impatient-looking people are waiting, being in such a locale can feel almost like being an appreciated guest in someone's home for an afternoon or evening.

The public areas of many outlets maximize visibility, thus making passers-by aware of what's going on inside as a way to encourage entry. However, an investigation center will need to create a balance between having enough visibility and also providing enough privacy from prying eyes.

I'm reminded of that need for balance by two restaurants near the free and low-cost concerts. I long avoided going into either one because I could see very little or nothing of their interiors from the sidewalk. After many years of striding past both, I finally entered one of them after noticing some other men my age having dinner there. In subsequent years, I continued to avoid the other restaurant, one whose interior is totally hidden from outside. Then, one day the restaurant I had been visiting was closed, and I had no choice but to try the other one if I wanted to watch the big game. I was pleasantly surprised to find that the food, service, and atmosphere were much better here than at the establishment I had been frequenting. The result was that my hanging-out habits drastically changed. Had this this second restaurant provided a little more visibility I would have been eating there many years sooner.

Why is some privacy attractive for an investigation center to provide? Women especially can receive unwelcome attention in public places. People with physical disabilities or unusual features can draw stares. If someone stops to peer at such individuals from outside, the visitor's discomfort can quickly become extreme. For the same reasons, it's also good to have cozy, less visible places inside that help reduce similarly unwelcome eyeing of visitors by others who are there.

Assuming that enough space is available and can be afforded, increasing the variety of hanging-out space will be quite desirable. For instance, one person's idea of a comfortable room might feel too open to someone else. Another individual's cozy cave might feel claustrophobic to another person. What is available within each area could also be varied so that those from different age groups and with varying interests would naturally gravitate to one place or another. For instance, an indoor play area for youngsters might be located next to where parents would enjoy gathering while keeping an eye on their offspring.

Flexibility in space use is also a good idea. Perhaps some areas could be converted for different hanging-out purposes throughout the day or week, depending on who is likely to be hanging out there. Making such a conversion might only require shifting some furniture and wall hangings, as well as changing the background music.

Scheduling events in better ways can also increase use of hanging-out space. For instance, having free lessons in checkers or chess for youngsters the first thing on Saturday morning might lead some to keep playing one another after the lesson at the center. If the center offered other games the youngsters would enjoy, perhaps a whole morning might be happily spent playing at a center. By attracting the youngsters and making appropriate programming choices available for their elders, it's likely that some parents, grandparents, and possibly even older siblings would decide it was better to attend appealing programs or to hang out at the center, instead of running errands or hanging out elsewhere.

Staff and volunteers should be encouraged to interact with visitors in ways that increase hanging out. Any approach used should seek to make the center feel as welcoming as the most hospitable home that a visitor has encountered. For instance, if beverages are available, new visitors should be given a free one, at least for the first visit. The center might also provide free beverages for anyone who brings in new visitors, so that they can enjoy some time hanging out together. If enough space is available, visitors might be provided opportunities to reserve either quieter private or small areas for more focused activities and discussions. Staff and volunteers might donate good books they no longer need to form a library for visitors to read from while at the center.

Some people might object that such an approach could fill an investigation center with homeless people seeking warmth in winter and coolness in summer. Well, God loves homeless people as much as He loves those who have homes. Such hanging out should also be encouraged. Having programs that can help homeless people get a grip on some of their personal issues might be beneficial, such as individual reading classes for those who need to gain more skills in order to get a job.

In doing so, some centers may find that homeless visitors discourage some others from returning, especially if the homeless people ask others for money while there. In planning the layout of the center and the ways that someone can hang out, it will be good to provide enough choices so that everyone will feel welcome and comfortable ... regardless of their attitudes towards and experiences with other people while there.

As you can appreciate, each center may need to be quite different from every other one to best serve the hanging-out needs of those who are most likely to visit. Avoid creating cookie-cutter centers except when the available space is very limited, and such concentration improves what kinds of and how much hanging out can be offered to visitors.

We look next at making investigation centers entertaining, another important aspect of increasing appeal.

Lesson Seventeen Assignments

1. How has hanging out helped people you know to try something new and absorb valuable lessons?

2. How could investigation centers become better hangouts in ways that would greatly increase how many people learn?

3. What other ways of being a good hangout do you think could attract more learners?

4. How might investigation centers be improved by becoming hangouts for visitors in seldom-available ways?

5. How has a hangout enabled you to learn and accomplish more than you otherwise would?

6. Which of the ways in which a hangout has helped you to learn and achieve more should be provided to others?

7. How should the center use being a hangout to attract and retain the support of more volunteers, staff, neighbors, suppliers, donors, founders, and other stakeholders?

Lesson Eighteen:

Entertaining

In that region there was an estate
of the leading citizen of the island,
whose name was Publius, who received us
and entertained us courteously for three days.
And it happened that the father of Publius
lay sick of a fever and dysentery.
Paul went in to him and prayed, and
he laid his hands on him and healed him.
So when this was done,
the rest of those on the island who had diseases
also came and were healed.

— Acts 28:7-9 (NKJV)

"Entertaining" has two meanings that are relevant for increasing the appeal of investigation centers. First, the word means being a good host or hostess who provides food, beverages, and possibly shelter in a courteous, friendly, and generous manner. That first meaning is captured by the example of Publius found in Acts 28:7-9 (NKJV). Second, "entertaining" means we find doing something to be pleasantly amusing or diverting. I'm sure that those who had never seen a miraculous healing found it entertaining in this sense to watch Paul heal diseased people on Malta.

Applying the first meaning of entertaining is valuable for establishing the right atmosphere for visitors at an investigation center. Think about the experiences you usually have at a public place. Except for the largest discount outlets and the most expensive restaurants, no one is likely to greet you as you enter. Even in these locales, the "greeter" may come across as someone who is more sizing you up as a potential shoplifter or tipper than someone who is serving as a host or hostess welcoming a valued visitor.

Obviously, a well-funded center can do more to offer hospitality than can one that's operating on a shoestring, but certainly any center can have a volunteer warmly step up and welcome a visitor. In doing so, avoid giving visitors the sense that there's a hidden agenda, such as "signing up" them up for activities, events, or programs. Instead, focus just on getting to know the person, as you would anyone you first meet who is looking for friendly help. As Jesus might remind us, treat the visitor as you would like to be treated, as someone God loves as much as He loves you.

As one model for what to do, I recently observed the actions of a woman whose approach impressed me. She not only greeted families as they arrived to participate in various activities and to attend some events, but she also walked with each family to show them where the various activities and events were located. In doing so, the woman stayed with each family until the members were well settled with other volunteers who were conducting the activities and events. Only after the family members stopped focusing on the woman did she say good-bye and head back to the door to repeat the welcoming service for yet another family.

Why did I like this approach so much? Well, I watched the faces of the families she helped and compared them to the faces of those who were merely given directions for where to go. While each kind of "greeting" was done in similarly friendly style, those who were escorted looked relaxed, eager, and happy. In contrast, the others looked wary, concerned, and more than a little tense as they headed off on their own.

The Bible tells about some of the differences that Jesus experienced in being received. In one home, no one did anything special for Him until a woman who was considered by that community to be a sinner bent down to wash His feet with her tears, then wiped them dry with her hair, followed by kissing His feet and anointing them with fragrant oil. When the "host" complained that Jesus was permitting this act to occur, Jesus rebuked the man for what he had not done as a host (Luke 7:36-50, NKJV). While I don't think that being hospitable means we need to do as much for the visitors at investigation centers as this woman did, it is quite clear that doing more than what is expected, as a kind and loving host or hostess might, is the right way to treat such visitors.

Let's now turn to the second meaning of "entertaining" for investigation centers: being amusing or diverting. By "amusing," I don't mean humorous. Rather, I mean "enjoyable enough" that we keep doing whatever it is. When something entertains us in this way, we stay involved longer than planned, simply due to enjoying the experience. Electronic games often have this effect on people. For example, a couple once complained to me about having sore arms, elbows, and backs after playing Wii for many hours on a console they had just acquired. My female friend said, "I just couldn't get enough." However, a limitation should be applied: This form of being entertaining must not distract people from growing closer to God.

If there can be a fun element while engaging in what the investigation center does for expanding and improving God's Kingdom, such fun can be part of a solid foundation for visitors happily spending many hours there. In thinking about what that experience could be like, I'm reminded of two two-year-old children who were watching television for the first time. These youngsters barely moved or breathed as they drank in each new visual element of the educational program. At any other time, these children would have, instead, been busily disassembling whatever was in the area.

Consider any classes you may have taken. If yours were at all like mine, you usually sat in a poorly ventilated room fighting off sleep as someone talked on and on about something that had little or no relevance to anything that interested you ... other than earning a decent grade for the course.

I contrast such boring teaching with the many "hands-on" seminars I've taken that included engaging in physical metaphors for the subject that was being covered, a great way to more powerfully bring home the ultimate message. I vividly remember such experiences and the lessons they taught, even though I can barely remember the names of any professors who lectured to me in college or graduate school. I also remember well those small classes where I engaged in discussions with the professor or instructor. Having so much focus on me (and my questions and responses) was truly unforgettable, and also much more educationally effective than I appreciated at the time.

So what do these observations suggest about ways that activities, events, and programs should be conducted at an investigation center? To me, it seems as if all forms of participation should provide either individual attention or group activities that include substantial physical and verbal interplay. On some occasions, it may be possible to do both. Wouldn't that be great?

One of my former students has made a nice success of combining individual and group interaction in her teaching. Let me describe how she does so. Her business offers dance and fitness classes. To make ballet more entertaining for her young students, she employs friendly helpers who constantly move through a class smiling and making small adjustments for each student. For her adult fitness students, my former student frequently changes the types of fitness offered, both in terms of what kinds of classes are available and what is done during each class. By keeping an eye on each student, friendly individual assistance is then provided that improves how effectively the exercises are done. For those who don't want to leave home to exercise, she also offers "virtual" classes where the instructor directs a handful of students over Skype, providing similar individual direction and feedback. Each online student can also see the other students, which permits some "group" interaction even though the individuals are apart. In many ways, her approach exemplifies some of what can be done to make investigation centers more entertaining.

By the way, dance and exercise classes are quite popular, as are the previously described cooking classes. Chances are that a successful investigation center will eventually offer dance, exercise, or cooking activities, classes, courses, and programs. Many people would also like to teach dance, exercise, and cooking, but they often cannot do so because of having a full-time job or school work, or being parents. An investigation center should be appealing to such potential instructors by making space available and attracting students who could be taught part-time. The center could better serve visitors by auditioning potential instructors to select those who are most entertaining and helpful while working with students.

Parents often look for enriching weekend, after-school, and vacation activities for their children. An investigation center can likewise draw on a substantial body of professionals who now teach or have previously taught various subjects, such as art, crafts, math, reading, and science. Volunteers and staff could again winnow the talent pool to bring in those with the most entertaining approaches. Those who teach could also be encouraged to share ideas with one another for improving their entertaining qualities. In addition, investigation centers could share information about videos, books, and other materials that previous visitors have found to be entertaining. If there is enough interest, classes for different skill levels could be established, enabling students to gain more appropriate support for engaging in their interests.

Would entertaining in these ways draw more people to an investigation center? I think so. As evidence, I recently stopped at a locale with the potential to provide many elements of what an investigation center might do. I arrived early one Saturday morning. While the center had capacity for easily handling hundreds of visitors, there were only about a hundred people there. Of this hundred, all but about ten people were either parents or their young children who had come for art classes.

From this example, I think it becomes clear that an investigation center won't have to provide very many different kinds of activities, courses, events, and programs to attract a full house of visitors. Instead, a good approach will often be to specialize in certain subjects and activities so that potential visitors associate the location with such entertaining opportunities.

By emphasizing the quality of being entertaining in this lesson, I don't mean to suggest that there should be any compromise in how helpful the services are in other dimensions. I see adding entertainment as a way to increase how many visitors attend, as well as by how much visitors feel they have benefited from the engagement. When those two results are achieved, undoubtedly the frequency of engagement by visitors will also be higher. With frequent enough involvement, visitors will then make connections with staff, volunteers, and other visitors that will increase the center's attractiveness as a hangout, our Lesson Seventeen topic.

As to the importance of entertainment, let me share a partial example, one that might be familiar to many readers. I'm reminded of the way that suburban YMCAs often use their space for family, as well as child-centered, activities that keep their facilities fully occupied for much of the day and night throughout the week. Some of the largest facilities include exercise and weight rooms, basketball courts, indoor running tracks, swimming pools, and dance studios, as well as places where parents and youngsters can attend individual classes and programs on a variety of subjects. While these organizations have an obviously Christian foundation, I noticed that many non-Christians attended a YMCA near my suburban home while my sons were young. Such attendance simply reflected the attractiveness of what was going on at this YMCA. Boys whose parents weren't believers would mercilessly pester their parents until permission was received to become part of a basketball team, learn karate, or gain a lifesaving certificate. Undoubtedly, the Holy Spirit was helping to make their appeals harder to resist.

Because I'm sure you have a good sense of what's entertaining, simply from engaging in your own interests, let's leave this subject for now.

In the next lesson, we take up adding do-it-yourself elements to an investigation center.

Lesson Eighteen Assignments

1. How have entertaining qualities helped people you know to try something new and absorb valuable lessons?

2. How could investigation centers become more entertaining in ways that would greatly increase how many people learn?

3. What other ways of being entertaining do you think could attract more learners?

4. How might investigation centers be improved by entertaining visitors in seldom-available ways?

5. How has something being entertaining enabled you to learn and accomplish more than you otherwise would?

6. Which of the ways that something being more entertaining has helped you to learn and achieve more should be provided to others?

7. How should the center use being more entertaining to attract and retain the support of more volunteers, staff, neighbors, suppliers, donors, founders, and other stakeholders?

Lesson Nineteen:

Do-It-Yourself

Do you have faith?
Have it to yourself before God.

— Romans 14:22 (NKJV)

The context for Romans 14:22 (NKJV) concerns what food a believer does or doesn't eat. The Apostle Paul explained here how one's faith should not be visible in any ways that would become a spiritual stumbling block to someone else. Paul was telling believers to focus on doing whatever exhibits peacefulness in relationships with fellow Christians: Be completely open with God, but watch what you do when other believers are around so that you don't divide the Body of Christ.

We should love God as well as all other people. While most of us would like to have the maximum freedom to do whatever they please, there are two important limits on doing so. One limit is defined by what opposes God. The other limit is where exercising God's permissible freedom either directly or indirectly damages people who are (or should be) in God's Kingdom ... such as by creating divisions among believers and discouraging nonbelievers from approaching God. In this lesson, keep these limits in mind as we consider how being able to "do it yourself" can attract and retain the involvement of more visitors, as well as increase the benefits received.

Do-it-yourself can make possible an experience that is customized, individual, and rare, qualities that can increase appeal. For retaining visitors, such qualities of do-it-yourself could sometimes increase satisfaction with what occurs at a center. Since do-it-yourself is often less expensive to provide than the alternatives, any resulting cost reductions might permit supplying either greater benefits to the current visitors, or the same benefits to an increased number of visitors.

Do-it-yourself has a bad reputation with some people, reminding them of the times when they or a family member attempted a task without proper training and tools ... resulting in a lot of unneeded effort and a poor result. Such a circumstance makes me recall times when I banged my thumb with a hammer while trying to strike a nail that needed to go into an awkward place. I also remember times when people bought furniture that had to be assembled ... which then proved to be all but impossible to accomplish. Some people cavalierly throw essential directions away ... and end up with either too many or too few pieces. When you think about such examples, how could do-it-yourself possibly be an advantage?

To gain advantages, I suggest simplifying do-it-yourself to avoid disasters while retaining as many as possible of the potential benefits. Let me explain a way to do so through an example. At a restaurant my daughter likes, the areas around the grills in the middle of the dining area are filled with beautifully prepared ingredients, sauces, and spices. Diners pick out the ingredients, sauces, and spices they want, and then combine and cook them to their personal satisfaction. While I'm no chef, I have been able to produce meals there that tasted superior to what I had experienced elsewhere. Once the food was perfectly prepared, I took it immediately to my seat so I could eat it at optimum temperature, another advantage over places that leave food sitting under inadequate heat lamps that dry out my meal while it grows cold. Keep in mind, however, that if the restaurant had not simplified the experience of do-it-yourself for me, I could have ended up with a mess.

So think of do-it-yourself as also being a way to obtain more benefits, rather than as only being a cause of disasters. Naturally, in some cases people will need help with do-it-yourself to obtain the right benefits and avoid bad results.

Here's an example of what I mean by helping people. An artist friend of mine teaches painting and sculpture. I once attended his workshop for making sculptures. While we mostly worked on our own, my friend had brought wonderful materials that we could include in our sculptures. While my art teacher in junior high school had only once given any of my art work a grade higher than a B, on this occasion I was able to use the well-selected materials to create a sculpture that I still enjoy ... unlike every other art work I have ever produced. Without those materials, I'm sure that I would have just had another forgettable flop.

Let me outline a few important aspects of this example. First, my friend knew that he shouldn't give us too narrow a set of choices. Some teachers might have, instead, provided each of us with a single coat hanger and said, "Go to it." Second, he appreciated that we needed something to get us started. By his choice of materials (much as the excellent, well-prepared ingredients provided at the restaurant helped turn me into an acceptable "chef" ... at least for myself), he allowed us to benefit from his imagination. Third, he wisely didn't interfere. He walked around talking to us about whatever we wanted to discuss. His observations were always encouraging. In my case, he remembered that I love the work of the artist Joan Miró before observing, "You've made your own Miró." In response, I beamed. Wouldn't you?

From this example, you can see how do-it-yourself can be successfully incorporated into learning situations. In doing so, I favor allowing visitors to set their own learning goals. God has graciously done that for me in several cases where I didn't begin to perceive the full potential fruitfulness of what He was calling me to do (such as during the early days of The 400 Year Project, to demonstrate ways to accelerate by at least 20 times the rate of all forms of global improvement). As a result of His gracious treatment, I have felt more comfortable taking on a new — and what I felt to be a very difficult — task. Visitors to investigation center should feel that same sense of comfort. As a result, some visitors will be willing to take on more fruitful tasks, surprising themselves by the unexpectedly substantial results they achieve.

I also favor allowing visitors a choice of ways to accomplish their goals. This flexibility works well because people can select methods that better fit their skills and preferences. In addition, as a result of making choices about methods, visitors will usually be more committed to making the selected methods work.

After choosing goals and methods, some visitors will be more encouraged and persistent if they can engage with others they enjoy being with. Observing others, learning from their reactions, and assisting others makes doing something new become more like an adventure or fun, rather than like doing something "difficult" or "challenging." While most of us like safe adventures and fun, fewer people like difficult and challenging tasks. By choosing with whom they engage in do-it-yourself activities, visitors will often be more relaxed and have a better experience while doing so. Because of these benefits, better approaches and more effort are likely to be applied.

Naturally, the activity's site will affect the desirability of applying do-it-yourself methods. For instance, put a somewhat unpleasant activity in a very desirable place, and the benefits of being there will often more than offset any unpleasantness associated with the activity. The reverse will often be true, as well.

Let me describe an example of what an ideal do-it-yourself learning experience might be like. Imagine that you wanted to enter the world's largest and most beautiful garden, one that is brimming with lovely flowers that flood the air with delightful fragrances, as well as with delicious, ripe fruits waiting to be picked and eaten. However, the garden is totally surrounded by a ten-foot-high wall many miles long that keeps you from entering. Got it?

Okay, a difficult do-it-yourself project would give you no resources and provide no directions other than pointing towards the wall. That doesn't sound like a good way to encourage visitors, does it?

So let's, instead, tell visitors that there might be places where trees hang large, strong limbs over the wall that extend into the garden. If a visitor went around the outside of the wall and found such a tree, the visitor could try climbing the tree. If that were possible, the top of the wall might be crossed over such a limb, but there could still be quite a drop from the limb to reach the garden floor.

That approach doesn't sound like it includes enough assistance, does it? Next to such a tree, let's place a long, stout rope where it will be easy to see. Surely, some visitors will figure out that they can climb the tree, cross over the wall on a limb, tie the rope to the limb, and climb carefully down the rope into the garden.

For someone with imagination, strength, and agility, that's certainly a doable approach. However, not everyone is gifted in these three ways.

Because of such individual limitations, a good do-it-yourself project would provide some alternate ways to enter the garden. One such alternate could be placing a light twelve-foot ladder in one area near the wall. Someone with good strength and balance could use the ladder to climb to the top of the wall, then straddle the top, pull the ladder to the top while still straddling it, then place the ladder securely against the garden side of the wall, and finally climb down the ladder into the garden.

Achieving such a result might still be beyond what some weak and smaller individuals could accomplish by themselves. So a well-designed, do-it-yourself project should add yet another alternative. Such a choice might involve building a gate that could be opened after successfully answering a riddle. Assuming the riddle wasn't too hard and visitors could help one another, such an alternative might help those who are good at solving riddles.

Unfortunately, I fear that there would still be some people left outside the garden. These individuals might also be given the address of a Web site where they could find other people who needed help or wanted to provide assistance for entering the garden. By using the Web site, teams could be assembled that could work together to get over the wall. A team might use the skills and knowledge of individual members to find and perform all aspects of what is required to enter the garden, making up for the individual weaknesses of other team members. For instance, a strong person on a team could do all aspects of handling the ladder from atop the wall so that each other member could simply use the ladder to first climb up the outside of the wall and then down the inside.

If you think about this example, I'm sure it will remind you of the sculpture class. The helpful choices are abundant, but the useful resources narrow the choices down to a manageable number. In doing so, individuals can accomplish the desired result without needing direction from the person who organized the task, activity, or event.

Naturally, I would be remiss if I did not point out that do-it-yourself projects can also add an element of intriguing entertainment for those involved by leading the visitor through some planned exciting experiences that reveal information, develop skills, and provide a sense of accomplishment. To explain this observation, let me use a different example.

In this case, imagine that you have to complete a 100,000-piece jigsaw puzzle without seeing a picture of the finished result. Just the sheer number of pieces might keep many people from starting.

However, now imagine that by putting together clusters of 500 related pieces (a typical number of pieces for a jigsaw puzzle) clues would be revealed that would make it easier to put together still other clusters of 500 related pieces. Such clues might refer to the image involved, suggest short-cut solutions, or permit obtaining information from other puzzle solvers. If organized in this way, solving the puzzle would be more tantalizing, seem more doable, and provide a larger number of experiences with developing insights that would furnish the puzzle solver with a sense of accomplishment at several points in putting the puzzle pieces together.

If all this solving could be tied in to also gaining some important kinds of insights, knowledge, or information that an individual independently wanted, rather than just for putting together the jigsaw puzzle, the incentive would be quite large for a visitor to stay focused and make progress.

Hopefully, these examples have given you a sense of how adding do-it-yourself elements to the investigation center's activities, classes, events, experiences, and programs can be used to increase the number of visitors, as well as how often they return.

In Lesson Twenty, we explore how to make an investigation center more appealing to visitors by providing a buffet of attractive options.

Lesson Nineteen Assignments

1. How have do-it-yourself elements helped people you know to try something new and absorb valuable lessons?

2. How could investigation centers make greater use of do-it-yourself approaches to significantly increase how many people learn?

3. What other ways of offering do-it-yourself choices could attract more learners?

4. How might investigation centers be improved by giving visitors do-it-yourself experiences in seldom-available and highly desirable ways?

5. How have do-it-yourself activities enabled you to learn and accomplish more than you otherwise would have?

6. Which of the ways that do-it-yourself activities have helped you to learn and achieve more should be provided to others?

7. How should the center provide more do-it-yourself options to attract and retain the support of more volunteers, staff, neighbors, suppliers, donors, founders, and other stakeholders?

Lesson Twenty:

Buffet

The LORD of hosts will make for all people
A feast of choice pieces,
A feast of wines on the lees,
Of fat things full of marrow,
Of well-refined wines on the lees.

And He will destroy on this mountain
The surface of the covering cast over all people,
And the veil that is spread over all nations.
He will swallow up death forever,
And the Lord GOD will wipe away tears from all faces;
The rebuke of His people
He will take away from all the earth;
For the LORD has spoken.

And it will be said in that day:

"Behold, this is our God;
We have waited for Him, and He will save us.
This is the LORD;
We have waited for Him;
We will be glad and rejoice in His salvation."

— Isaiah 25:6-9 (NKJV)

Isaiah 25:6-9 (NKJV) describes, in part, how the LORD will reform the Earth by providing choice food and wines, taking death away forever, and wiping away all the tears of saved people. Isn't it interesting that great eating and drinking are mentioned first as what God will provide before referring to the far more consequential spiritual, physical, and emotional benefits of Salvation, the end of death, and consoling those who are sad? Keep that set of future benefits in mind as we consider ways to improve an investigation center's fruitfulness for visitors by operating more like a buffet does in a restaurant, at a catered event, or during a neighborhood party.

The word "buffet" when pronounced with a hard "t" also means to physically toss around or to be hit by a blow or shock, and when the "t" is silent the word refers to a sideboard or counter from which diners fill their plates with food. However, we are focusing, instead, on the eating aspect of the softer sounding version of buffet: *a meal* in which the guests serve themselves. With this last meaning, many people associate the characteristics of having a large quantity of food, perhaps even a bounteous amount, as well as more than the usual number of food choices.

When I picture such a buffet, I remember brunch with my family at a wonderful restaurant on my last birthday where I served myself as much as I wanted (and as often as I wanted) from dozens of tasty food items and delicious beverages, spread in heaping piles and filled-to-the-brim containers on six long tables. While the other diners were far from malnourished, most of them sampled the choices with as much gusto as if they had just missed a meal or two.

Some people prefer tasting as many foods as possible during a meal. To make such tasting easier when there is no buffet, some families and cultures follow a custom of offering a portion of any item from their individual plates to everyone else, especially when there are many dessert choices. For such sweet delights, enjoying some of each dessert's great flavor and richness without actually consuming as many calories as there are in a whole dessert portion is an obvious advantage for those who are watching their weight.

For me, a buffet's advantages include avoiding food and beverage choices I don't like without being obvious in doing so. If, instead, I attend a meal where everyone has the same items on a plate, it can be hard to avoid showing that I did not consume those uncooked, snail-encrusted, caramel-filled grasshoppers that the hostess is so delighted to provide. Consequently, at a buffet I eat with less concern about offending whoever picked the menu or prepared the meal. In such cases, my enjoyment is improved by more tranquil dining.

At a buffet, it's usually considered okay to return for more food or beverages without waiting for others to finish their plates. In most such circumstances, however, the polite thing to do is to ask if any of the others would like you to bring back something for them. When dining with very slow eaters, or those who are more interested in talking than eating, such flexibility can be very valuable for anyone who is feeling quite hungry. Naturally, such flexibility is far superior to being at any restaurant where the service is slower than you prefer.

While I could go on to list still more benefits of a buffet, I'm going to stop after mentioning just one more: cost savings. Due to serving larger numbers of people who usually take only the quantity they intend to eat, the percentage of food that is wasted will often be reduced over what would occur if each person were served identical amounts. In addition, there don't need to be as many people serving the food, further cutting costs.

How might all such advantages be made available for an investigation center's visitors? Providing a wider variety of choices in activities, classes, courses, events, experiences, and programs is an obvious application. By doing so, a center could increase its appeal to those with such various interests.

However, adult education programs often practice this same approach and don't succeed. Why? It's because their programs must attract a minimum number of students so that it's affordable to provide an offered option. To be the best "buffet" of alternatives for visitors, an investigation center will need to be able to provide an option to anyone, even if that person is the only one who wants it.

How might such provision be made more affordable for the center and its visitors? Most adult education programs have two large costs that affect their ability to provide choices to a single individual: sharing information about choices through advertising and program brochures, and paying instructors. If letting current and potential visitors know about the choices is done primarily by electronic means and word-of-mouth, the cost of sharing information can be kept quite a bit lower. If the instructors are all volunteers, the salary cost can be eliminated.

In taking this approach, there are some problems to consider. For instance, many instructors only want to do classroom teaching and would be uncomfortable working with only one student. A possible solution is to attract, as well, tutors who normally provide one-on-one and small-group instruction. While many tutors primarily work for pay, most of them also provide at least some free or low-cost tutoring to those who need help, but cannot afford to pay. Such generosity is especially likely to be found among those instructors and tutors who are either young or retired.

Another technique could reduce costs while still involving those who prefer to teach larger groups: Have master teachers prepare video-based programs that visitors could mostly study on their own, while the center provides as-needed access to someone to answer questions and suggest improvements in a student's approach. The gratification of serving many more people in this way would attract, I'm sure, at least some master teachers to participate for either no pay or a small stipend.

Another possibility is offering Skype-based courses, such as Lesson Eighteen describes concerning exercise classes. By doing so, several centers could pool the interests of visitors to provide a teaching opportunity that would attract an instructor, whether as a volunteer or for affordable pay, who could even work from home if the instructor so desired.

Another possible dimension of being more buffet-like is offering a variety of ways to engage in any individual activity, class, course, event, experience, or program. While many organizations provide a choice of where to sit during events, performances, and programs (mostly as a way to obtain more income from attendees), the buffet approach would mean actually providing quite different ways to engage or participate.

Here's an example. Let's assume that an investigation center offers cooking classes. A visitor who wanted a full experience with the least personal effort could have an individual lesson at home using ingredients brought by the instructor. Obviously, there would be a charge for doing so. A less individualized version of such a lesson would offer the same teaching in someone's home, but for a group of the visitor's friends. An event like this could be a part of a social occasion that would include eating the meal afterward. Options in either case could include tasting various kinds of beer or wine.

Such a lesson could also be held at the instructor's residence or restaurant, especially where doing so would make the experience more interesting. For example, some restaurants now provide dining tables in their kitchens so that food preparation can be studied in detail while enjoying a meal.

Naturally, the lesson could also occur at the center, especially when few, if any, special facilities or equipment are needed. While there, options could include taking the class but not eating the food, or being able to just purchase a meal prepared during the lesson without taking the lesson.

Of course, the lesson could also be conducted via video, or live by Skype. Options to have the ingredients delivered to the visitor's home could be offered.

Many people have fairly unusual learning styles, or deal with disabilities that require special types of instruction. By sharing a large base of potential instructors, tutors, and instruction requests, nearby centers would be potentially able to accommodate many more special requirements, something that would greatly increase the value of such offerings. By providing information about what nearby investigation centers are doing, a center could also expand awareness of choices for visitors, even if they have no special needs, so that they would be more likely to obtain what they need at one place or another.

Even when classes are not involved, programs would be more beneficial for some by providing sign language translations for the deaf, as well as spoken translations for those who only know languages rarely used in the programs. Where culturally based misunderstandings are likely, any activity, class, course, event, experience, or program would be enhanced by providing advance explanations of what is about to occur so that any such misunderstandings might be avoided.

Naturally, providing so many choices, as long as they are economical, would attract and enable a great many more people to participate in more enjoyable ways.

I could go on to expand the concept of being more like a buffet through varying a center's offerings, but I'm sure you can see how such flexibility (especially after there are many centers in an area) would enable a center to provide a buffet of choices that would be even more tempting and satisfying than the birthday buffet that I so much enjoyed last year.

In Lesson Twenty-One, we look at making an investigation center "sticky" in the positive sense of how so-called superglue allows two items to be permanently bonded together after applying very little time, money, and effort.

Lesson Twenty Assignments

1. How have adding choices and making them more accessible helped people you know to try new things and absorb valuable lessons?

2. How could investigation centers make greater use of buffet-style choices to significantly increase how many people learn?

3. What other ways of offering buffet-style choices could attract more learners?

4. How might investigation centers be improved by giving visitors buffet-like experiences in seldom-available ways?

5. How has having buffet-like choices enabled you to learn and accomplish more than you otherwise would have?

6. Which of the ways for providing buffet-like variety that helped you to learn and achieve more should be provided to others?

7. How should the center provide more buffet-type options to attract and retain the support of more volunteers, staff, neighbors, suppliers, donors, founders, and other stakeholders?

Lesson Twenty-One:

Sticky

A man who has friends must himself be friendly,
But there is a friend who sticks closer than a brother.

— Proverbs 18:24 (NKJV)

Proverbs 18:24 (NKJV) describes one good way of being sticky: staying in close contact with someone, regardless of what is happening in that person's life. Such loyalty is appreciated by almost everyone. Fortunately, sticking close to believers through thick and thin is an attribute of our wonderful Lord and Savior, Jesus Christ, the Shepherd who stays with us even in the valley of the shadow of death and leads us beside the still waters (Psalm 23, NKJV). In addition, behaving loyally is what most spouses promise to one another, often referred to during a marriage ceremony as taking a spouse for better or for worse, as well as in sickness and in health.

In everyday life, there are obviously two sides to a relationship or personal connection being sticky. When we desire someone or something to be connected or available, stickiness is great. However, when we don't want such a connection, being sticky can bring us messy, annoying consequences. Just consider women beset by stalkers, for example.

In the context of investigation centers, however, there are few downsides to visitors being permanently connected to the place and its activities. Only if the visitors are habitual criminals who prey on other visitors should permanent connections cause harm.

Of course, some visitors are going to be more difficult to serve than are others. The center's staff and volunteers should deal with any related challenges by serving in those instances with as much love, kindness, and patience as possible, as Jesus directed us to do. In doing so, we will expand and improve God's Kingdom, in part by becoming more like Jesus.

While so-called superglue is a fine example of a quick and easy way to make a long-lasting connection between two objects, the relationship of a thrill-seeker to a bungee cord is a better analogy for what an investigation center should seek to accomplish with visitors. Let me first explain what I'm referring to with regard to a bungee cord. For a thrill (or a terrifying event, depending on your perspective), few things in life can match jumping off the center of a high bridge while only connected by an elastic cord to avoid falling to a fatal end. After the downward motion is arrested, the jumper bobs up and down several times until the cord is wheeled in, pulling the jumper up to the launching point on the bridge.

Let me now explain what I have in mind in comparing a bungee cord's elastic connection to such a jumper to an investigation center's ideal relationship with a visitor. Instead of a bungee cord being the connection, knowledge-seeking visitors will stay in touch due to their interests in and memories of enjoying activities, classes, courses, events, experiences, and programs at the center, such that visitors will often think about returning to the center. The visitors' memories of what occurred at the center will serve as the bungee cord that keeps them from falling into harm in daily life and then pulls them back to the center for more good experiences. For nonbelievers who come to faith in Jesus and the Gospel, learning at the center will, in fact, save them from being spiritually dead, similar to the way that a bungee cord will keep a jumper safe from physically dying.

While all organizations attempt to increase involvement of stake-holders by building positive experiences, few organizations are very successful in establishing any long-term involvements with those they serve. Such poor results do not occur for lack of incentives: For instance, companies that make such a connection with a customer earn higher profits and cash flow. However, in attempting to gain these benefits, businesses have to contend with customers becoming tired of the business's offerings and finding better offerings elsewhere.

How can an investigation center be more successful in maintaining its connections with visitors than other organizations are with those that they serve? There's a powerful force for sticking with an investigation center that is usually absent from being involved with most secular organizations: the Holy Spirit. For a center that effectively helps nonbelievers to learn more about God and believers to draw closer to Him, the Holy Spirit will powerfully remind such people about the most fruitful activities to engage in at the center and encourage their participation.

How can a center become more fruitful by building on the Holy Spirit's influence? Prayer is the best way to find such answers, especially by listening to God, but let me also suggest some possibilities here ... while encouraging you to pray for guidance about whether His will is for you to engage in any of these possibilities.

Helping visitors to have more spiritual experiences is one possible way for an investigation center to become more fruitful for the Lord. Just look at the potential effects on believers. While a great many churches do a fine job of providing opportunities to worship, teaching through sermons, and encouraging Godly service, many churches do not perform equally well in providing spiritual experiences. As a simple example, many believers have never been taught either the importance of having an extended daily quiet time with God or what to do during such time. Even for those who have been so taught, many believers know only one way of doing so. Consequently, other ways of engaging in spiritual experiences during quiet times remain unexplored, even including such obvious ones as having extended, silent retreats with God.

In addition, my impression is that some believers have not yet had serving experiences that have brought them very much closer to God. Serving is, of course, one way that believers can directly bear fruit for God's Kingdom. However, some forms of service are more likely than are others to spiritually develop the server. For instance, greeting people when they arrive (a worthy thing to do) isn't going to expand one's spiritual awareness and depth nearly as much as is providing more personal assistance, such as by helping a disabled person to participate in an activity that greatly improves his or her spiritual connection to God.

Investigation centers can add spiritual experiences to any of their activities, classes, courses, events, and programs. Since not everyone (especially nonbelievers) will want to have spiritual experiences, such involvement may often need to be offered as an option to an activity, class, course, event, or program. However, if the spiritual experience is well described, merely receiving that information could amplify the Holy Spirit's influence in encouraging a believer to participate. After better appreciating what's involved in such an experience, some nonbelievers who are seeking God may also respond to such a call by the Holy Spirit.

Offering spiritual experiences that supplement many regular activities people already enjoy can be another good way to develop such stickiness through the Holy Spirit. In this way, preferences and habits for doing something can quickly become connected to preferences and habits for also having spiritual experiences. Here's an example. Many people like to hike in beautiful surroundings, gaining benefits such as fresh air, exercise, lovely sights, companionship, and a change from tiresome routines. Most people take occasional rest breaks while hiking. What if hikes were planned so that their stopping places were coincident with ideal spots for silent meditation on various aspects of who God is? Were that to occur, hikers would be more likely to remain thinking about God while heading to the next stopping point, rather than mulling over more mundane subjects. Each such hike could be developed to employ a different spiritual theme. By doing so, a hiker could later create her or his own versions of the experience, even while hiking alone without any direction from an investigation center ... thus forming a fruitful habit of using hikes to gain spiritual experiences and knowledge.

While more could be said about adding spiritual experiences, keep in mind that spiritual experiences themselves could be provided independently of doing any other activity. For instance, the church I attend offers soul-care retreats three times a year that are three to six hours in length. I find such retreats to be so refreshing and helpful for my spiritual development that I also seek out other retreat opportunities, sometimes including ones lasting as long as three days. Clearly, engaging in such retreats has proven to be quite sticky for me.

Another form of stickiness is doing something with a person you are fond of being with, especially if the person is your spouse, sibling, relative, or good friend. If you both enjoy the engagement (or even if it's just a good way to be together), the two of you are more likely to attend the next occasion when the activity is available. An investigation center could encourage such stickiness by developing its service offerings to be more desirable when done with another person.

A related form of stickiness is developing an attachment to those who either teach or are involved in providing an investigation center's offerings. By engaging especially appealing or admired individuals to volunteer or work at the centers, the desirable qualities of the individuals can help open visitors' minds to trying something that would otherwise have been perceived as being uninteresting, irrelevant, or even undesirable. I see this characteristic all in the time in my own reading and activities. When people I admire and appreciate direct something, I'll often get involved even if I have no good reason to think that such engagement will have any other benefits.

Still another way to increase stickiness is by involving those who have done an activity in the past to help deliver the same or a similar activity. Many people are pleased to have a chance to experience the same activity, but from a different vantage point by having either a leadership or supporting role. For those who undertake specific responsibilities, fruitful opportunities to serve God can be experienced that could feel especially satisfying.

For those who are having trouble finding a paying job, an investigation center could also help them to develop knowledge, skill, experience, and credibility for performing such work. For instance, such a job track could be created by working with an organization that wants more candidates for hard-to-fill positions. In some cases, the sponsoring firm might even offer its own facilities for engaging in job preparation, along with its personnel to be the instructors.

Sometimes an investigation center may be able to offer activities, classes, courses, events, experiences, and programs that involve serving extremely appealing people. For instance, many people like to help their children and grandchildren. A program that provides an opportunity to learn how to more effectively do so might be then followed by a different program during which those who took the first program practice more advanced ways of serving such children. Through time spent together at the center, the visitor and a child could easily become better bonded in a way that would lead them to return more frequently, especially if any other programs encouraged such involvement.

Well, I'm sure by now you can see the essence of how stickiness can be used to attract, retain, and increase the involvement of more visitors, especially in conjunction with the Holy Spirit. It is time now to consider our next lesson: Genuine.

Lesson Twenty-One Assignments

1. How has some person, place, or thing providing stickiness helped people you know to try something new and learn valuable lessons?

2. How could investigation centers use being sticky to significantly increase how many people learn?

3. What other ways of being sticky could attract more learners?

4. How might investigation centers be improved by being sticky in seldom-available ways?

5. How has stickiness enabled you to learn and accomplish more than you otherwise would have?

6. Which of the ways for being sticky that helped you to learn and achieve more should be provided to others?

7. How should the center use being sticky to attract and retain the support of more volunteers, staff, neighbors, suppliers, donors, founders, and other stakeholders?

Lesson Twenty-Two:

Genuine

In this you greatly rejoice, though now for a little while,
if need be, you have been grieved by various trials,
that the genuineness of your faith,
being *much more precious than gold that perishes,*
though it is tested by fire,
may be found to praise, honor, and glory
at the revelation of Jesus Christ,
whom having not seen you love.
Though now you do not see Him, yet believing,
you rejoice with joy inexpressible and full of glory,
receiving the end of your faith — the salvation of your souls.

— 1 Peter 1:6-9 (NKJV)

A reference to something being genuine is found only twice in the New King James Version of the Bible, both times in terms of defining someone's faith in Jesus and the Gospel. In 1 Peter 1:6-9 (NKJV), the reference is to how trials, by testing our faith, can prove that our faith is genuine. To nonbelievers and some believers, that explanation for why individuals experience trials could seem quite strange in terms of what else they know about God. If He is supposed to love us, has a great plan for our lives, and wants the best for us, why would He test our faith by permitting grievous trials? Well, faith is what activates and deepens our relationship with God. While we are tried (and God promises not to try us beyond what we can endure), God is there to comfort us and give us peace. He will also bring the trials to a close when our faith has been taken to the next level that He intends, a level that enables us to have a better relationship with Him.

Because so many companies seem fascinated with reducing costs, obtaining genuine products can be even harder to accomplish than finding genuine faith. For instance, the next time your vehicle needs a part, you might find that your local repair station will use any part for the repair ... except a replacement part from the vehicle's manufacturer. As one extreme of lowering their costs, producers who are not totally honest may also copy genuine offerings in ways that seek to fool buyers and casual observers into accepting something false as being genuine. Visit the quickly spread blanket of a street vendor in almost any city, and you'll be offered what appear to be items identical to those that cost a great deal more. For people who are into pretense, making such a purchase can be satisfying. However, when someone wants the article to work well or last a long time, disappointment is sure to follow.

Let's look more closely at faith. Do you think anyone wants to follow a god who isn't the genuine article? If there are such people, I have yet to meet one. Such individuals should only anticipate disappointment. Instead, people are usually convinced that the god they follow is genuine. And the list of gods that can be followed is remarkably long. Because of there being so many choices, all the believers in these various gods cannot possibly be right. Such a circumstance suggests that it's easy for people to make a mistake when assessing the spiritual realm.

While many people have trouble telling the difference between what is spiritually genuine and false, virtually everyone can tell the difference between someone who is behaving in a genuinely helpful way and someone else who is just going through the motions. One way to help visitors develop genuine faith is by serving them in the most authentically loving and considerate ways, the ways that Jesus demonstrated, encouraged, and commanded. When such behavior is founded in the server's genuine faith in Him, those whose faith isn't yet genuine might notice the difference between how they treat others and how much better they are treated at an investigation center. Having such an experience will undoubtedly draw some individuals to want to learn more about God. By then providing genuine ways to experience God, an investigation center can help someone seeking an initial or a better relationship with God to come closer to gaining one or to actually have such a relationship.

As discussed in prior lessons, many churches don't often teach about having or provide spiritual experiences beyond whatever God furnishes through His own initiative in the sanctuary, the Sunday school classroom, or a church activity designed for some other purpose. By providing visitors with a variety of spiritual experiences, an investigation center can become a great resource for helping believers and nonbelievers experience God in the most genuine and rewarding ways.

Investigation centers should also provide activities, classes, courses, events, experiences, and programs that will help visitors to develop better relations with other people. While many would like to have more and better relationships with others, some appear not to know very effective ways to do so.

An experience yesterday reminded me of how unintended problems can be caused by lacking such knowledge. A man I've gotten to know a little over the last few years spent some time with me so we could become better acquainted. I welcomed his openness while we did so, seeing this as an opportunity to develop our relationship. I was honored by his candor in describing the good, the bad, and the ugly about his past. At the same time, I was struck as he did so that there was a kind of reverse pride being demonstrated. He was trying to impress me through relating these stories, especially ones about how bad his behavior had been.

Well, the experiences spoke for themselves. Like all of us, he had made some mistakes, realized his errors, and stopped doing those things. I applauded his commitment and ability to do so. My own difficulties in stopping certain kinds of mistakes make me appreciate all the more when others successfully do so.

However, his need to impress me put up a barrier to further developing our relationship. Ironically, I would have been quite impressed if he *hadn't* tried to impress me, just because he had turned his life around to such an extent. So while his purpose in trying to impress was to bring us together, in doing so he was actually keeping us apart.

Why? Well, I found it difficult to respond in a positive way to the obvious hints that I should be impressed at various points ... because I wasn't impressed, and I didn't want to give him any false encouragement. So I sat there silent at times when he expected me to provide an "Attaboy!"

I doubt if he realized the effect that he was having on me. I could tell he was puzzled by my passivity. Had he known my reactions, I'm sure he would have spoken differently.

Like all of us, he was having trouble seeing what was in front of him ... even though no one else could have missed it! In the meantime, I am praying about how to share my reactions in a loving and kind way at the right time so that we can draw closer together.

Staff and volunteers need to practice being more genuine with one another and the visitors. Otherwise, honest desires to do the right thing may misfire, as happened in the example I just described.

Keep in mind that the Bible and the Holy Spirit are much better sources of instruction than I am about how to be genuine in showing God's love to others. However, to get your thinking started, let me share some impressions I have gained while instructing others about how to develop their personal relationships. First, focus solely on the other person, leaving yourself and your own desires aside. Keep in mind the parable of the Good Samaritan. In Luke 10:30-37 (NKJV), the Good Samaritan neither sought nor gained any tangible benefits from assisting the naked, half-dead man. In fact, the Good Samaritan experienced just the opposite in terms of tangible effects: He was delayed, inconvenienced by having to walk rather than to ride, probably lost sleep tending the man, and had expenses associated with providing aid on the road and at the inn. Whatever Earthly rewards the Good Samaritan received were simply related to knowing that he had done the right thing and was following God's will.

Second, developing a relationship depends on taking actions, not just promising to act. As the Bible relates, actions tell us more reliably what someone really believes and thinks than what the person says. Some people may promise you anything and deliver nothing. Others may promise little, if anything, but always keep their word. The parable of the Good Samaritan includes no reports of promises made by him to the injured man, but certainly contains many helpful actions. Notice that the Good Samaritan was concerned about more than just the injured man: The Good Samaritan also promised to repay the innkeeper for the costs of any unexpected care required by the wounded man, keeping the innkeeper from being harmed ... while also improving the likelihood that the wounded man would receive all the care that he needed, care that the Good Samaritan may not have been in a position to personally provide.

Third, whatever is done should be intended to increase or improve God's Kingdom. Drawing someone closer to God is one way to do so. Improving how much someone else or you become like Jesus is another way.

So let's look at ways these three elements (focusing on others, acting, and aiming to increase or improve God's Kingdom) might be merged at an investigation center. Obviously, the center should be operated for the benefit of all the visitors, and everything done there must reflect that focus. However, doing so doesn't mean that other stakeholders (such as volunteers, staff, neighbors, suppliers, donors, and founders) are irrelevant and should be ignored in this regard. All stakeholders should be treated with dignity, love, kindness, and compassion, as well as be provided with any needed support. Otherwise, Christ-like qualities will not be demonstrated by serving visitors. The most important action during an investigation center's day will often occur before the doors open and the first visitor arrives, as the staff and volunteers meet to pray, seek God's guidance, and encourage one another in serving. Such sessions may be similar to how worship and teaching teams spiritually prepare before a church service.

Visitors should also be made aware of what to expect at the center before being served. Otherwise, someone might interpret an attempt to help as being inappropriate. Some organizations explain the values they seek to honor, in part, by prominently posting them. What could be more appropriate than to share some relevant Bible verses that capture the heart of what Jesus wants done?

When charges for services are required, it's only natural to expect that newer visitors will want to pay as little as possible, as well as be suspicious of any requests for payment. Consequently, it will be valuable to offer many activities to new visitors at no charge. How to fund such costs, should there be any, is a topic that Part Four addresses. Even after visitors feel comfortable that charges are reasonable, efforts should be made to keep costs low for them.

Most people are also sensitive about how others approach them. Being known and called by name in person is usually perceived as being a friendly way to be greeted, as long as strangers do not overhear what is said. Not receiving unwanted contacts is also important, whether by telephone, e-mail, or in person. Since people vary in how they want to be approached, it's good to ask each visitor his or her preferences and then to remember and honor them.

While we could go through quite a long list of do's and don'ts, I think it's more important to just focus on employing two practices: Tell people you want them to let you know if you aren't acting in a genuine way that they appreciate, and apologize with a humble heart and spirit whenever you become aware of having possibly made a mistake. There is no better way to be genuine than by letting others know you are only human and want to make amends when you do the wrong thing (or fail to do the right one).

We turn next to the final lesson in this part: Peaceful.

Lesson Twenty-Two Assignments

1. How has some person, place, or thing being genuine helped people you know to try something new and learn valuable lessons?

2. How could investigation centers make greater use of being genuine to significantly increase how many people learn?

3. What other ways of being genuine could attract more learners?

4. How might investigation centers be improved by being genuine in seldom-available ways?

5. How has genuineness enabled you to learn and accomplish more than you otherwise would have?

6. Which of the ways for being genuine that helped you to learn and achieve more should be provided to others?

7. How should the center use being genuine to attract and retain the support of more volunteers, staff, neighbors, suppliers, donors, founders, and other stakeholders?

Lesson Twenty-Three:

Peaceful

Then justice will dwell in the wilderness,
And righteousness remain in the fruitful field.
The work of righteousness will be peace,
And the effect of righteousness,
quietness and assurance forever.
My people will dwell in a peaceful habitation,
In secure dwellings, and in quiet resting places,
Though hail comes down on the forest,
And the city is brought low in humiliation.
Blessed are you who sow beside all waters,
Who send out freely the feet of the ox and the donkey.

— Isaiah 32:16-20 (NKJV)

Isaiah 32:16-20 (NKJV) describes what God's reign will be like when Jesus returns. Justice will prevail, even in the wilderness, while there will be righteousness where the people dwell. And the work of such righteousness will be creating peace, with the effect of bringing quiet and assurance forever. The last four lines suggest that His peace will prevail, even in the midst of adverse effects, due to believers being in a relationship with Him. One result is that we will be able to freely engage in meeting our material needs, no matter what else is going on.

Peace is never more yearned for than while in the midst of strife. How soon, however, we can surrender such peaceful yearnings to

179

seek "justice" for some cause, relinquishing in the process the peace we have "learned" to take for granted! Fortunately, God knows how to give us true peace, peace that comes from repenting our sins, believing in Jesus Christ, being in a personal relationship with Him, and casting our cares, worries, and problems on Him and relying on His infinite and loving capabilities.

Understanding how someone can experience peace in the midst of terrible difficulties is one of the most difficult lessons for seekers and new believers to grasp. However, those who are in such difficulties and don't yet believe in or rely on Him will sometimes be attracted by the promise of gaining peacefulness, even if some practical struggles persist.

With God's help, an investigation center can be an island that provides such peace, one that can help nonbelievers and not-as-yet-mature believers understand and eventually be filled with true and lasting peace. Let's explore how this result might be accomplished.

I recently visited a place that imbued me with a sense of peace greater than I had recently felt in similar sites. Let me describe the location and a little about the experience. First, the site was far away from all but a few buildings and roads. If you looked in most directions, you only saw God's beautiful creation. Such places are becoming harder to find in the urban and suburban parts of many developed countries. Second, it was quiet there. Even when people were present, they walked and spoke quietly. The buildings were totally soundproof so that noise didn't leak from elsewhere to wherever I was inside at the time. Third, if I passed someone, she or he gave me a relaxed, pleasant smile, seeming to invite me into conversation ... if I wished. Those who worked there often stopped unbidden to gently point out some interesting feature of where I was, doing so in a kind way that did not feel intrusive. Fourth, when I entered a building to look at something or to ask a question, people smiled as though they were glad to see me and offered to help me ... often anticipating my question or need to immediately provide exactly what was most useful. Fifth, there was no clutter. Sixth, there was always plenty of room for me to do whatever I wanted ... either with others or by myself.

After leaving, I also thought a little about what could have made this place even more peaceful. While the site and how the people there behaved certainly reflected God's love, God was mostly missing ... except for the presence of His creation. Places to rest where Bibles were open to thought-provoking or informative verses would have drawn me closer to Him. Bible verses might also have been inscribed on some walls. If those verses had described or reflected on His peace, I would have been more often reminded of Him and how He provides peace. Some of those who didn't know that God offers peace might have found the same verses to be instructive and very encouraging.

More pleasant sounds could have been added. Some sort of subdued white noise could have made me feel even more relaxed. I was reminded of such potential while sitting in some of the meditation areas at our church during Holy Week, spaces that featured running water that nicely mimicked the sound of a burbling brook. While there, I was reminded of the times when my family stayed overnight in oceanfront communities where the gentle washing of waves outside put me into deeper slumber than I have since experienced.

At the location I've been describing, I was left to my own devices to decide what to do. As a result, someone could have found more peace if she or he had already known how to seek it. However, if someone was troubled, there was no obvious source for helping to move from that state into a more peaceful one. In fact, if a person had been feeling troubled, he or she might have left, due to feeling that she or he didn't belong in this place where everyone seemed quite mellow, while personally feeling ready to scream in frustration.

The visitor center at this location contained materials that very thoroughly described whatever activities, classes, courses, events, and programs were scheduled. However, I was disappointed to see that children's classes comprised almost all of what was then available. There was literally no activity scheduled that day in which I could have participated to gain peace. Nor was there any such activity scheduled for all but an occasional few hours in the future. From the perspective of someone who wanted engagement of some sort during a visit, this location provided little more than what could be accessed by visiting a neighborhood park solely equipped with benches.

As a way to test my observations about adding peacefulness to a location, think about where you enjoy visiting. Then, think about how well each place helps you gain more peace. I'm sure you'll find that peace is seldom available outside of some quiet place outdoors that has a beautiful view or a part of your home where you can be undisturbed when you want to refresh your spirit.

Providing ways for troubled people to gain peace is difficult. Doing so can even be at odds with most other ways of serving visitors. As a result, any investigation center that wants to help people be more peaceful should focus part of the site on this purpose. While doing so, be careful not to try to do too many things in the same space. The area that serves as a place for silent retreats cannot simultaneously serve as the location for classes in how to experience more of God's peace. If you must use the same space for multiple purposes related to gaining peace, while scheduling keep in mind the times of the day and night when visitors are most likely to want one or the other kind of help with gaining peacefulness.

Balancing the needs of those who want to do boisterous, noisy activities with those who want to feel as if they are walking alone in the wilderness will be a particularly difficult challenge for an investigation center. Sound insulation can do only so much in this regard. Physical separation may be essential. For this reason, the physical site for an ideal investigation center may need to be large and diverse enough in its types of space so that a full range of activities is possible without infringing on whatever anyone else is doing. Where less space is available, a center may have to choose whether to emphasize providing peacefulness or some of the more active benefits.

In the eight lessons in this part, we have considered some remarkable models for providing the qualities that can make an investigation center more fruitful in serving visitors and other stakeholders. Chances are that you are now wondering how so many things can be accomplished in one location. Keeping in mind that only God is perfect, we will now look in Part Four at how to follow His directions for expanding and improving His Kingdom by providing visitors with information, knowledge, and experiences through adding many helpful investigation centers.

Lesson Twenty-Three Assignments

1. How has some person, place, or thing being peaceful helped people you know to try something new and learn valuable lessons?

2. How could investigation centers make greater use of being peaceful to significantly increase how many people learn?

3. What other ways of being peaceful could attract more learners?

4. How might investigation centers be improved by being peaceful in seldom-available ways?

5. How has peacefulness enabled you to learn and accomplish more than you otherwise would have?

6. Which of the ways for being peaceful that helped you to learn and achieve more should be provided to others?

7. How should the center use being peaceful to attract and retain the support of more volunteers, staff, neighbors, suppliers, donors, founders, and other stakeholders?

Part Four:

Combine Models

"I pray for them. I do not pray for the world
but for those whom You have given Me,
for they are Yours.
And all Mine are Yours, and Yours are Mine,
and I am glorified in them.
Now I am no longer in the world,
but these are in the world, and I come to You.
Holy Father, keep through Your name
those whom You have given Me,
that they may be one as We are.*"*

— John 17:9-11 (NKJV)

In John 17:9-11 (NKJV), Jesus prayed for believers to be unified, as Jesus and His Father are. Investigation centers can help accomplish this result for believers. One way is by paying attention to the wisdom of unification in combining potential models for establishing and operating an investigation center.

In Part Four, our focus is on what might seem to some to be an impossible task: merging the various models outlined in Part Three's lessons to enable an investigation center to meet more of the needs Part One describes through supplying those qualities Part Two discusses. Let me start with a word of advice: Relax! God will help you to appreciate and do what He wants, serving as a perfect resource for whatever is needed. Also, realize that no two investigation centers are going to be serving the same kinds of visitors in identical ways. As a result, you may not need to combine all of the models. Finally, consider that how an investigation center starts its operations will undoubtedly be quite a bit simpler than how it will ultimately operate. Feel free to start small and simple, while keeping the flexibility to do more in the due time of God's will. Consider that Jesus made the prayer in John 17:9-11 (NKJV) at a time when there were few believers in Him as the Messiah. We, too, should keep the end in mind as we work to accomplish what should be done in the present.

We turn first in this part to setting goals for an investigation center, the subject contained in Lesson Twenty-Four. You will need the Holy Spirit's guidance here because we are limited and fallible, while God is the opposite. While you may be feeling excited about the possibilities of what can be done by providing a large number of investigation centers that serve many kinds of visitors in a substantial number of ways, your initial goals will probably not include doing very many of such things. Instead, it's good to be led by the Holy Spirit to set appropriate goals for what can be done initially in just a few superb ways, ways that will be highly effective in expanding and improving God's Kingdom.

In fact, the less you try to do at first, the more you may accomplish in the long run. Here's an example. While an investigation center's founders might be intrigued by the potential to apply all eight models described in Part Three in one location, such an approach could lead to making mistakes that would harm credibility in ways from which it would be hard to recover. If, instead, a center first attempts to implement only part of one model, while retaining great flexibility to do more in the future, many more visitors may be attracted, stay involved with the center, and be drawn closer to God.

With appropriate initial goals in place, you will be ready to prepare a breakthrough in effectively providing services through an investigation center. Since this center will be operating through a new organization, it will be easy to make mistakes. If conventional planning and implementation methods are used, results may also be slow to develop and modest in scope and impact. In Lesson Twenty-Five, we draw on the work and experience of The 400 Year Project to identify the most appropriate methods for planning and implementing a breakthrough in an investigation center's effectiveness so that it can eventually become a greater source of substantial spiritual improvement for a large number of visitors.

Once operating, an investigation center needs to pay attention to what's working well and what isn't, as well as to how visitors react to what they experience and wish they could do there. Such close attention to learning from visitor expectations and the actual experiences at a center should inform improving the initial model, as well as doing the same for any subsequent, enhanced models. Making the improvements is our subject in Lesson Twenty-Six. Those who are involved in making such assessments and improvements can again apply the information contained in Lesson Twenty-Five to identify the best breakthrough methods to use.

The more successful an investigation center is, the easier it will be for those who operate it to become complacent about what they are doing. When that happens, it's as though someone first loved Jesus with all of his or her heart, mind, and soul, but later substituted merely singing hymns for engaging with Him in such complete love. As the rebukes aimed at five of the seven churches named in the book of Revelation reveal, our complete love of Jesus and desire to draw closer to Him should always be at the heart of everything we do. In Lesson Twenty-Seven, we discuss how continuing to learn should inform improving whatever is done at an investigation center.

We turn next to Lesson Twenty-Four: Set Goals.

Lesson Twenty-Four:

Set Goals

Not that I have already attained, or am already perfected;
but I press on, that I may lay hold of that
for which Christ Jesus has also laid hold of me.
Brethren, I do not count myself to have apprehended;
but one thing I do, forgetting those things which are behind
and reaching forward to those things which are ahead,
I press toward the goal for the prize
of the upward call of God in Christ Jesus.

— Philippians 3:12-14 (NKJV)

The Apostle Paul's words in Philippians 3:12-14 (NKJV) are an excellent reminder that any goals set for an investigation center should be consistent with what God wants to accomplish for His Kingdom. To learn what God's purposes are for the investigation center you intend to start or help operate, seek His guidance in prayer and pay careful attention to what He tells you through the Holy Spirit, Bible verses you read, His creation, what other Christians say and do, circumstances you experience, what you sense in your heart, and any other supernatural means.

While only God can inform you through these methods, understanding His directions can sometimes be much improved by asking Him questions. In this lesson, I outline what some useful questions might be in relation to a center's goals. For those who are familiar with The 400 Year Project's writings about business-model innovation (especially as described in *The Ultimate Competitive Advantage*, Berrett-Koehler, 2003), some of this lesson's questions may seem familiar. I draw on the seven dimensions of such improvements (*who, what, when, why, where, how,* and *how much*) to develop the questions included here. If you aren't familiar with this kind of thinking, I intend for this lesson's content to be self-explanatory for informing your prayers about appropriate goals for starting and operating an investigation center.

Before looking at the seven dimensions, let me observe that the goals God initially directs you to may be quite different from what He will later want you to pursue. For instance, while I was engaged in The 400 Year Project (to find and demonstrate ways to accelerate the rate of global improvements in all dimensions of human endeavor, from the spiritual to the material) from 1995 through 2015, God continually kept me directed at just taking the next short steps ... without even hinting about any of the steps to follow. I suspect He might do the same with regard to developing new investigation centers. Otherwise, the scope of what will need to be done could seem overwhelming to our limited minds. We are fortunate that He sees the big picture over the long term so that each little thing He directs us to do ultimately leads to accomplishing something mighty for His Kingdom.

Although you could ask God if His directions are just intended for the near-term, realize that you might not receive an immediate answer to that question. He might delay answering to make you more comfortable with doing just what He initially wants.

We now turn our attention to the questions you might ask God. You could begin by asking *who should be served?* The answer could come back as broad as being everyone in a certain geographical area, or as narrow as being just a certain type of person who lives in one building. In the latter case, God might know that highly appealing, convenient facilities could be easily borrowed just for serving such people. For instance, in a housing project with a community center, space might be earmarked for educating children after school, yet no such programs might be currently operating. Simply offering to do so could make such space available at no cost. In the case of being directed to serve many people in a large area, God may know of several ways to access different facilities at little or zero cost and with minimal effort that would attract many visitors.

While it is not often useful to speculate about God's reasons for what He does, I have found that it helps people to bow to His superior wisdom by thinking a bit about some possible reasons why God might start in one direction, rather than another. In terms of choosing those who will first be served, God might be considering how influential these people can be in attracting others to an investigation center. For example, if my grandchildren want to take courses at a certain place, I'm going to visit and check out those classes before they enroll. In the process, I might find out about a class or course that I, too, should be taking. If so, helping my grandchildren might be a great way to gain my attention and participation.

Once you know who should be served, it's time to ask a second question, *who should serve them?* As you can easily imagine, attempting to answer this question without initially identifying who will be served would make little sense, except for centers that will initially be seeking to serve almost everyone in a wide variety of ways. However, for centers with a narrower focus, this second question cannot be fully answered until more is known about the center. Of course, God already has all of this figured out. We look next at a question that can help you to know His will.

The third question is *what should be done for serving these people?* Throughout this book, I have focused on how investigation centers might provide various activities, classes, courses, events, experiences, and programs. However, occasionally centers may simply play the role of being where some desirable attributes, such as peacefulness, are more often experienced. The circumstances and needs of those who are served will obviously play a large role in determining what will be most helpful to provide for them. With these characteristics clarified, you can then think more clearly about who should serve visitors and better understand God's directions in this regard.

After that, you need to learn from God *when should visitors be served?* The answer obviously depends on the times such visitors are most available and willing to come to a center. The availability of locations at various times on different days may also play a role.

Another valuable question to ask God is *why will visitors want to be served?* Such reasons will obviously inform choices of locations, service offerings, providers, and operating times.

With these perspectives in mind, it will become easier to understand God's directions for *where should an investigation center provide its services?* As earlier lessons make clear, I hope, a center may provide offerings in more than one location. In fact, there may be no locations that are fully dedicated to the center's use, but rather a series of places where space is borrowed for slivers of time to serve people who are already at the location. For instance, most libraries have rooms where small meetings could be held. For many topics, these rooms might be borrowed to provide appealing services for many of the people who regularly visit libraries. Similarly, senior centers often have such facilities. Some nursery schools and after-school care services are located in church-provided buildings that are well away from the church premises. Such facilities might be equally available for investigation-center activities during times when other activities are not being held. Employers who want to train more potential employees might also make parts of their job sites available for such purposes.

After so many aspects of what a center should do are understood, it becomes more obvious *how should visitors be served?* In doing so, appeal and effectiveness should be balanced, as I am sure God will direct, so that more could be accomplished for His Kingdom. With experience, insights can be developed for improving how visitors are served. Experiments with alternate methods can also indicate what kinds of changes to make.

In previous lessons, I promised to address financing investigation centers later. To begin that consideration, let's consider the related topic of *how much should visitors pay?* Even quite modest charges can reduce how many people engage in an activity. For something that few people initially appreciate has any value, visitor reluctance will be all the greater. Consider, too, that I've been to some pretty amazing places where I had tremendous experiences at no cost ... and yet I was the only one there taking advantage of the resources.

If centers are going to focus on having visitors pay little, then they are going to either need many resources or to keep costs very low. To understand what to do, ask God *what should be the budget for the investigation center and how should the funds be spent?* In answering, God will undoubtedly address different kinds of expenses. For instance, in some of the cases where facility and operating costs will be low or zero, funds may still be needed to inform potential visitors about the services or no one will make use of the center's offerings.

All of such considerations eventually feed into the question of *how should financial and other resources be obtained?* In the next few paragraphs, I share some thoughts that I hope will be useful to you.

Consistently throughout The 400 Year Project, I asked God if He wanted me to raise substantial sums to do things that He had directed, or to make do with little. He always chose the latter alternative. I don't believe it was because He is stingy or could not have provided more. Instead, I'm reminded of Jesus sending out the first 12 disciples, and later 70 others, with instructions to take with them no staff, bag, food, money, or extra clothes (as described in Luke 9:3 and 10:4, NKJV). While Bible commentators have proposed many reasons for these instructions, surely Jesus was using such directions as a way to increase the faith of these men so they would rely more on God and less on material resources.

Consider the alternative. If believers have unlimited sums available, they might begin to rely on such a storehouse of wealth to do whatever they pleased, rather than seeking to please God so that He would continue to provide the essentials.

So, unless God tells you to spend a great deal and promises to provide what you need to do so, you should probably assume that He wants you to be a good steward of a very few resources you cannot do without. After you make good use of such resources, He may decide to provide you with more, as Jesus described in the parable of the minas (Luke 19:11-27, NKJV).

Doing much with little is also a way that you can demonstrate to visitors that God is great. I'm sure visitors will also be happier to pay for services after seeing how effectively the center is making use of very few resources.

If you are going to be working with very limited resources, ask God to show you how to deliver services on a shoestring with just a few visitors before expanding what you offer. Otherwise, you might misgauge what is required and disappoint visitors by providing less than what they expect and need.

I also recommend that you pray to God for direction concerning *when should the center start operating?* Otherwise, you might repeat the mistake I did concerning this book and delay beginning. Having until recently been negligent in this regard, I can certainly attest that being directed to do something that initially seems incomprehensible can seem to the natural mind like a good reason to delay. Instead, view what you are being asked to do as an opportunity to rely more on God. He will provide anything you need: from directions to resources. In the course of experiencing His provision, your faith will grow in delightful ways. After you succeed with His help, He will probably reward you with some even more interesting and spiritually challenging tasks.

Let me leave you with one final caution: Don't try to set these goals independently of Him. While you may be quite capable and skilled, He will do it better. Trust Him!

In Lesson Twenty-Five, we look next at how to accomplish these goals by choosing the correct breakthrough process for becoming a highly fruitful investigation center.

Lesson Twenty-Four Assignments

1. Who should be served by this investigation center?

2. Who should serve these visitors?

3. What should be done for serving the visitors?

4. When should visitors be served?

5. Where will the services be provided?

6. Why will visitors want such services?

7. How should the services be provided?

8. How much should visitors pay?

9. How much should the center spend?

10. How should any needed resources be obtained?

11. When should the investigation center start operating?

Lesson Twenty-Five:

Choose the Right Breakthrough Process

You did not choose Me,
but I chose you and appointed you
that you should go and bear fruit, and
that your fruit should remain,
that whatever you ask the Father in My name
He may give you.

— John 15:16 (NKJV)

In John 15:16 (NKJV), Jesus told His disciples that He had selected them for the purpose of being fruitful and that they had access to our Heavenly Father to receive whatever was required to be fruitful for the Kingdom by asking for it in His name. The same intent and provision are true for us today. Before the world was created, God developed a plan for each of us to be fruitful. If you have read this far and are feeling encouraged by what you have read, God may be sending you a message that being part of establishing or operating an investigation center is part of His plan for your life. What a blessing that Divine intention would be!

I focus in this lesson on choosing the right breakthrough process for initially establishing an investigation center. I do this simply because so many centers need to be founded. However, I will also refer to some ways to solve simpler problems, many of which are bound to arise during the operation of any investigation center.

While studying the Bible, you have probably noticed how God required those who became fruitful to do whatever they could do before He supplied the rest of what was required. As one example, consider Exodus 17 (NKJV). After God's people escaped from Pharaoh, they were still in the desert at Rephidim (where God had Moses strike a rock with the rod of God to bring forth water) when the Amalekites came to fight. While Joshua led the Hebrew troops, Moses held up the rod of God. When Moses did so, God's people outfought the enemy. If Moses put the rod down, the Amalekites were more successful than the Hebrews. To deal with Moses' weakness, Aaron and Hur held up Moses' tired hands and arms, and the Hebrews prevailed by the end of the day.

You might be wondering what God might be calling you to do as your part of establishing an investigation center. While I do not know the answer, I'm sure that there is one for all who are so called. Whatever that role is, performing it will bring Him glory and honor. Once again, be in prayer seeking His direction.

For some centers, God may have intended that the breakthrough processes of The 400 Year Project be applied to stretch resources and multiply effectiveness. While I don't know if you are supposed to use these processes, I do feel called by Him to share with you how these breakthrough processes might be applied. Another reason for addressing the processes here is that God may intend that some investigation centers train people to use these processes for His purposes.

Unfortunately, the available space in this book does not permit teaching you how to use each of the breakthrough processes. However, please realize that *Your Breakthroughs* (400 Year Project Press, 2016) is an inexpensive, condensed resource that contains a good outline of each breakthrough process. That book also describes which other 400 Year Project books encompass more detailed instructions, should you determine that a process is one that God intends for you to study and apply.

However, I can give you an overview here of the choices available for applying such breakthrough processes. We begin with *2,000 percent solutions: any method of accomplishing what you or your organization does now with 20 times more productivity, such as the current results being generated with less than 1/21 the present time, resources, and effort; or accomplishing 21 times as much or more, while employing the same or less time, resources, and effort; or any combination of accomplishing more and using less time, resources, and effort that amounts to at least a 20-times increase in effectiveness.*

Okay, now you've got the definition. What does it mean to be 20-times more productive? Let's look at an example: Assume that you now spend 5 hours a week reading necessary material for your work. Perhaps what you read are scientific or medical research articles, or updates on trends in your industry. A 2,000 percent solution would be to change your reading so that you could accomplish the same job results by only reading for 12 minutes a week. Such an improvement might be accomplished by a combination of improving reading speed, comprehension, and note taking. You might also delegate to others making preliminary scans of and summarizing the material to enable you to focus on just the most pertinent and valuable reading.

Here's an example of a personal 2,000 percent solution that was also an organizational 2,000 percent solution. The chief financial officer of a leading company spent over 100 working days a year heading up the firm's budgeting process. By delegating all but 3 days of that process to the controller, the CFO added 97 days to work on untapped corporate opportunities. While doing so, he also improved working relations with the other company leaders by not being in the middle of budgetary conflicts. As a result, the CFO helped facilitate operating changes that added tens of millions of dollars to annual company profits.

If you want to create 2,000 percent solutions, you'll find it helpful to first eliminate and delegate tasks that clutter your schedule so you will have time to work on this highly productive activity. Most 2,000 percent solutions can be developed with a total effort of 60 to

120 hours by one person. Split the effort across a team, and the individual time demands fall.

How available are 2,000 percent solutions? A corollary to Pareto's Law (referred to by many as the 80/20 principle, reflecting that 80 percent of the results can be observed to come from 20 percent of the people doing an activity) states that 80 percent of the results of any economic activity come from 20 percent or fewer of the efforts. By simply studying what the most effective people accomplish and then ideally combining their methods, the productivity of virtually any activity can be improved by at least 20 times.

If you reapply the 2,000 percent solution process to the same issue, you can exponentially increase benefits. For example, with a second such solution developed by repeating the process, benefits expand by 400 times. With a second repetition, benefits will then expand by 8,000 times. And so on.

What if 2,000 percent solutions could have multiplier effects on the size of benefits from 2,000 percent solutions for different aspects of what an individual or an organization does? Such results can be accomplished by using *complementary 2,000 percent solutions, ones that exponentially multiply the benefits of other 2,000 percent solutions.* Doing so is one feasible approach for many people to more quickly gain access to a highly effective investigation center. One 2,000 percent solution might reduce the costs of starting an investigation center by 96 percent from what would ordinarily happen. A complementary 2,000 percent solution might then reduce the costs of operating the center by 96 percent, as well. A third such solution might increase how many visitors engage by 20 times, while not increasing total costs. The result of three such solutions could be to increase how many people are served with the same resources by 8,000 times. One such combined solution might be enough to blanket a small American state with reasonably nearby investigation centers. Add just one more complementary solution, such as one that increases effectiveness in spiritually developing those who visit a center by 20 times, and the combination would probably be enough to cover an entire country with investigation centers while using few resources.

The good news is that even more can be accomplished in making breakthroughs: Develop and apply *excellent solutions*. Let me explain excellent solutions in terms of the other types of solutions we've just reviewed: *a single breakthrough solution that provides at least the same combined benefit expansion as ten complementary 2,000 percent solutions (or nine rounds of improvements to a 2,000 percent solution) under any set of external conditions, aided by unstoppable human reactions that speed the rate of implementation.* Think of such a solution as being like a 2,000 percent solution for making many complementary or repeated 2,000 percent solutions. That observation is true because an excellent solution requires only making one set of changes.

What could be accomplished with one excellent solution? Such a solution would contribute a single set of changes that would enable filling the world with highly effective investigation centers.

How might you decide which of these solutions to apply? Obviously, begin by praying. However, having some background information about solution choices might help you to better understand what God tells you to do.

If what you are called by God to accomplish involves few people and an increase in effectiveness that is less than 500 times, you can gain the results you want by simply applying and repeating the 2,000 percent solution process once or twice. Establishing a single, narrowly functioning investigation center might often be accomplished in this way.

If, instead, your calling is to affect hundreds or more people and to make effectiveness improve by more than 500 times, you can just repeat the 2,000 percent solution process to get there, but applying the right complementary 2,000 percent solutions will probably take you to your goal a little faster. Such an approach might work quite well for a single, broadly functioning investigation center.

In the alternative, if your calling will affect many thousands or more people and require increasing effectiveness by at least 3 million times, an excellent solution is probably a faster and a more reliable method. Such a calling might relate to establishing some sort of regional or national presence.

After praying and following God's guidance to work with one of these methods, read the pertinent sections of *Your Breakthroughs* and the most relevant books about implementing the methods. Then, develop an inventory of the skills and knowledge that you are missing in order to employ a given method. After that, consider the most effective ways to fill in for whatever is lacking, including:

- Reading more about the methods
- Partnering with people who have the appropriate skills or knowledge
- Working with an organization that has complementary capabilities
- Conducting new research
- Searching for future best practices to use for filling in your remaining lacks

Next, break down the steps you need to take into as many independent elements as possible for improving personal effectiveness, for eliminating stalls (bad thinking habits that delay improving), and for implementing the method or methods you'll be using to create a solution. After that, evaluate the best order for performing those elements so that the amount of work, the elapsed time, and the expense will be minimized.

Once you have those elements defined, further divide them into specific actions that are needed to accomplish each element. Doing so will help you avoid getting lost in a maze of steps and elements. Instead, you will be able to follow a list of daily actions and check them off after completion.

Applying a process well requires selecting dates for accomplishing the elements. However, since you don't have experience in doing some of these actions, it will be hard for you to know how long each one will take. So I suggest that you only assign completion dates to what you believe you can finish with the time and resources available over the next sixty days. In doing so, be sure to start taking timely actions where the work will require much longer than sixty days to complete. Then, regularly review the dates and adjust them to reflect your experience. Most people will make such reviews and adjustments weekly, but feel free to choose any frequency that makes sense to you.

To assess how appropriate your plans are before you actually begin taking these actions, review your steps, elements, and actions with others you will be working with or who have more experience. If you cannot find anyone else with whom to do so, I'll be happy to help you with your initial list. Just send me an e-mail to donmitchell@fastforward400.com/.

In providing this explanation, I have been addressing the people who like to start at the beginning and move logically to the end. I know that some people prefer to go from Z to A. I am sometimes one of them. For example, I like to read magazines and newspapers from the back to the front. Does that help you understand what I mean by Z to A?

For such individuals, the planning processes I've been describing would normally be conducted in the opposite order: Begin with a sense of what the result will look like in increased fruitfulness and then work backward in time through the process most likely to develop such a result to identify what impediments will have to be removed to overcome stalls (bad thinking habits), eliminate ignorance, neutralize mental baggage of other sorts, and change priorities. Such individuals will then be able to determine quite remarkable insights into what actions will make the biggest differences and will eventually establish a list of what to work on that will give all those actions much higher priority. I think the benefits of such thinking are potentially so substantial that I suggest the A to Z thinkers consider testing their intentions in this manner, in addition to what they did with developing a logical or chronological sequence.

Some few other individuals may also see some sort of connect-the-dots way through what needs to be done. What I mean here is that they can link from what is missing now to make the successful breakthrough to what isn't being done now, and then build a simple set of steps to get from one place to the other. This way of planning can also be quite effective. Once again, I commend it as an additional approach to those who normally prefer to use a different planning method.

Of course, many people will just be called to work on certain aspects of making a breakthrough, such as a part of its development or perhaps some element of its implementation. For these individuals, it will be valuable to orient any roles that can only begin after the work of others is done to what those other individuals have actually done. So there will be a need for these people to monitor key developments that determine the timing and shape of their roles. For those who will be working on the center's inception, the steps involved will be much like the ones for those who will be starting an excellent solution and then continuing it through a long implementation.

We turn next in Lesson Twenty-Six to developing the model of an investigation center after it begins operations.

Lesson Twenty-Five Assignments

1. What is your calling from God concerning investigation centers?

2. Which breakthrough method will work best for what you are called to accomplish?

3. What improvements in personal effectiveness do you need to make for accomplishing this calling?

4. What stalls (bad thinking habits) do you need to overcome for employing the breakthrough method?

5. What stalls do any organizations you will be working with need to overcome?

6. How will you organize the steps needed to accomplish your calling?

7. How will you manage to follow those steps?

8. What is your initial schedule for accomplishing actions in the next sixty days?

Lesson Twenty-Six:

Keep Improving the Model

The everlasting God, the LORD,
The Creator of the ends of the earth,
Neither faints nor is weary.
His understanding is unsearchable.
He gives power to the weak,
And to those who have *no might*
He increases strength.

Even the youths shall faint and be weary,
And the young men shall utterly fall,
But those who wait on the LORD
Shall renew their strength;
They shall mount up with wings like eagles,
They shall run and not be weary,
They shall walk and not faint.

— Isaiah 40:28-31 (NKJV)

In Isaiah 40:28-31 (NKJV), we find a profound reminder that God is eternal, never weakens, understands beyond what we do, and shares His power and strength with those who need them to do His will. As a result, those who do what God wants, when He wants, will be continually renewed in their strength and endurance to accomplish His purposes.

Some people might believe that there is little or nothing left to accomplish after a breakthrough solution has already helped establish a highly effective investigation center, or possibly even a number of them. Let's look at the most extreme case where an excellent solution has enhanced useful benefits being provided by 10 trillion times while using the same or less time, money, and effort.

In such a case, we would soon observe that a superabundance of one or a few benefits exposes other lacks, creating the potential to do more in related areas, much as initially planting more seeds ensures having many more seeds to plant in the future. As an example of this point, consider teaching beginning readers at investigation centers. Imagine that you have developed an excellent solution that advances youthful literacy for each of the Earth's children by thousands of times through a combination of increasing reading speed, comprehension, analytical skill, recall, and the ability to apply what is read. While such a result is mind-boggling in terms of its immense value, such a breakthrough would also lead to a shortage of age-appropriate materials for the youngsters who could now apply these enhanced abilities. If you then expand the excellent solution's goals to include increasing the quantity and quality of such materials by a huge margin, these youngsters' effectiveness in applying what they read could grow by additional thousands of times. Wow!

From this example, I'm sure you now better appreciate how circumstances can make it attractive to combine any breakthrough solution with an additional complementary breakthrough that greatly enhances the value of benefits, substantially increases necessary resources, or some combination of these two dimensions. Now, isn't exploring the practicality of such a result worth taking a bit of time to consider? I think so.

To do so obviously requires going back to basics by praying to God about what goals the investigation center should now be seeking to accomplish. Because of any successes that have occurred, such new directions will take into account new possibilities that were initially hidden from our eyes.

Let me point out a potential problem. Most people don't like to repeat what they did before. For example, the repetition of steps one through seven of the 2,000 percent solution process (the eighth step's direction) is more often skipped than performed. Because repeating of steps one through eight in the excellent-solution process calls for much more time and effort, I fear that more excellent-solution developers will also skip this ninth step than will perform it.

That's a big mistake: All those who have repeated the 2,000 percent solution process increased benefits by at least an additional 20 times, going from 20 times more productivity to 400 times more!

I suspect that repeating goal-setting can be similarly productive. Ecclesiastes 8:16-17 (NKJV) should caution us that regardless how hard, how far, or how broadly we search, God has already accomplished vastly more than we can ask, think, or understand. I imagine this circumstance to be something like the following analogy. Our current knowledge represents the equivalent of standing next to the top of a three-thousand-mile-high library that's almost totally buried in the ground. What we see is just a little point sticking out of the ground that is actually the point of the library's lightning rod. We aren't even close to entering the library. Can you imagine what we might learn should that happy entry occur?

While some people could take the pessimistic view that we will never open a door to access all the knowledge that God could provide, I disagree. If God reveals more extensive goals for investigation centers, in His own good time through His Holy Spirit He can also reveal to us any aspects of such hidden knowledge that serve His purposes in ways that we can use. Any remaining limitations then probably relate more to our willingness to serve His purposes with pure hearts than to His ability for making the knowledge usable.

Regardless of whether our limited minds can grasp and apply all of this unknown knowledge, we currently operate with such a tiny fragment of what there is to know that even advancing to gain a bigger, but a still minuscule, portion of what is there can bring mind-boggling benefits. Through the Holy Spirit revealing enhanced ways to make much greater use of our resources since 1995, God has been providing ever-greater glimpses of what such potential is. I believe that He's not done showing the way. Even now, I can almost touch a future so amazing that it will change nearly everything we believe we know, as well as what we think we must do.

Another reason to restart thinking what an investigation center does is that important opportunities may have been overlooked in developing the initial model. Ecclesiastes 7:9-12 (NKJV) reminds us to focus continually on what we should do differently, rather than wasting time regretting either what did or didn't take place in the past. The verses instruct us to combine wisdom with an inheritance that's illuminated by the sun. This advice could be interpreted as being sure to use what has happened to develop knowledge in light of wisdom from the Holy Spirit and the Bible. Let's look more closely at this interpretation.

At the end of major projects, I notice that some decisions I earlier considered to be unimportant actually have had large, unexpected consequences, such as when investigations were cut off that might have become highly beneficial. Many of such decisions were intended to focus more attention on what seemed to be more promising opportunities or to reduce work for the most valuable contributors. In such cases, a better decision would have been to slow the solution's development so that more high-potential investigations could have been completed during the initial work. As Ecclesiastes 7:9-12 (NKJV) directs, such experiences should only be used for improving performance, rather than for encouraging any complaints and finger pointing about what went wrong. Be sure that any promising lines of inquiry now receive more appropriate attention.

How might we identify highly promising lines of inquiry? Begin by conducting a project review that employs three different panels:

1. One panel consists of those who are interested in improving the investigation center's results, played little or no role in de-

veloping the center, don't operate it now, and are willing to be as constructively critical as possible of what was done.

2. Another panel contains visitors, staff, volunteers, and providers who played little or no role in starting the center and are interested in finding as many ways as possible to improve the center.

3. A third panel includes people who worked at the heart of establishing the center and are eager to comb through what was done to spot mistakes and missed opportunities, as well as to identify what is valuable to consider again.

Each panel should be able to access any information that individual members request (subject only to safeguards required for protecting privacy). Information provided to any panel member should be immediately shared with every other panel member. By such sharing, useful questions raised by one person will become more valuable by having more people thinking about them in the context of relevant information.

The three panels should report their findings to the others, as well as to an oversight group. Each panel should also be asked to comment about the findings of the other two panels for the benefit of the oversight group.

Everyone in the oversight group should have a key role for improving the model. I strongly urge you to select 60 to 70 percent of the oversight group from among those who will help lead the improvement process after playing small or no roles for establishing the center. The remaining 30 to 40 percent part of the group should comprise those who played major roles in starting the center and are known for their wisdom, as well as for their mentoring skills. Avoid selecting anyone for the oversight group who bullies or tries to dominate others.

The oversight group should also look beyond the panels to find useful suggestions. Others who were active during the center's development should be asked to comment on what is decided and done during the model-improvement process to ensure that any insights gained during the original work are remembered and appropriately considered. However, those who are leading the current round of improvements should have the final say about what is or isn't done. Otherwise, helpful communications might be turned into harmful restrictions that limit accomplishments.

After the panels and oversight group are established, specifically ask each member on at least four different occasions to suggest inquiries that should be addressed more thoroughly. If the oversight group shows substantial interest in expanding a specific inquiry, one or more teams should be assigned to focus just on that topic (or aspects thereof). Should many different people be able to contribute useful ideas and information, the oversight group should take a close look at whether it's appropriate to conduct one or more online contests during the early stages of the inquiries to help gain more ideas and information.

To reduce false steps, oversight group members and model-improvement leaders should clearly spell out the questions they want answered and the kinds of information they are seeking. I also encourage the oversight group members and model-improvement leaders to narrowly define what they hope to accomplish through seeking answers.

It's equally important that those working on such inquiries and online contests have freedom to expand on the assignments they receive without compromising what is provided. Otherwise, useful inquiries might be stifled.

Investigating entirely new questions can also be very productive. Let's think about ways to do so. As you can tell from the many Bible verses included in this book, I have found Scripture to be a constantly fruitful source for drawing my attention to important points that provide fertile soil in which the Holy Spirit has graciously cultivated my understanding. If one person can gain so many useful directions from Bible study and prayer, just think of how much more can be accomplished by an entire model-improvement team engaging in such seeking. Pray about how best to do so and for the repetition to be even more Spirit-led than the initial steps were.

Sometimes people who are not accustomed to looking for new questions have trouble starting. To help, let me share a brief list of possibilities. While I have no idea whether the items on this list are appropriate for improving your center's model, I invite you to pray and think about these items as a possible start for drawing your attention to beneficial, new inquiries:

- Ways to redress past injuries or wrongs
- Perpetual provisions for future needs
- Provisions so large that current unmet needs fall to zero and existing resources can be shifted into supplying other purposes
- Extraordinary provisions that greatly exceed immediate needs
- Provisions that replace more than all the resources currently being used
- Expanding current resources well beyond the original quantity
- Virtuous cycles of resource usage that lead to ever-expanding availability
- Virtuous cycles of ever-greater benefit increases
- Waste being turned into valuable resources

Many forms of understanding become much easier after we reach a new vantage point, such as by having just started an investigation center or visiting another one that successfully applies a quite different approach. Be sure to look for and remain open to finding and learning from such new vantage points.

We now shift to the book's final lesson: Continue Learning.

Lesson Twenty-Six Assignments

1. What is your calling from God for improving the models of investigation centers?

2. How can you ensure that model improvements will be continually sought?

3. What stalls (bad thinking habits) do you need to overcome for finding and making model improvements?

4. What stalls does the investigation center need to overcome?

5. What methods should be applied for making model improvements?

6. What is your initial schedule in the next sixty days for accomplishing the necessary actions to make model improvements?

Lesson Twenty-Seven:

Continue Learning

But God has revealed them to us through His Spirit.
For the Spirit searches all things, yes, the deep things of God.
For what man knows the things of a man
except the spirit of the man which is in him?
Even so no one knows the things of God except the Spirit of God.
Now we have received, not the spirit of the world,
but the Spirit who is from God,
that we might know the things
that have been freely given to us by God.

— 1 Corinthians 2:10-12 (NKJV)

However, when He, the Spirit of truth, has come,
He will guide you into all truth;
for He will not speak on His own authority,
but whatever He hears He will speak; and
He will tell you things to come.

— John 16:13 (NKJV)

I see the previous lessons in this book as being helpful for orienting those who have been called to establish and initially operate an investigation center. Such instructions for *what to do* and *how to do it* are much like teaching someone to read: introducing letters, adding

215

to vocabulary, laying out the rules of grammar, and so forth. However, to become an effective reader, other skills are also needed: selecting proper texts to read, testing the propositions they advance, and determining how to apply what is validated about the reading.

While developing the comparable, more advanced skills for improving an investigation center, producing more of its benefits, and better using what is provided, rules-based directions are less helpful. Such rules can easily distract from advancing the goals of the investigation center by shifting attention to achieving something like religious legalism or bureaucratic compliance.

Instead, an investigation center is best advanced by all involved submitting to God's will, especially as revealed by the Holy Spirit. The quotations from 1 Corinthians 2:10-12 (NKJV) and John 16:13 (NKJV) demonstrate the significance of having such reliance.

Let me give you an example of how harmful it can be to have too many rules. Some years ago, hospitals in the United States had the right to refuse service to patients who could not pay. In this environment, zealous hospital managers often developed complicated rules for determining whether a patient would receive treatment. In some cases, patients who could pay were denied care because they could not comply with the rules, such as when someone with health insurance had left proof at home or it had been lost during an accident. Many patients who needed immediate attention did not receive it, and some people died or were permanently disabled as a consequence. This problem was "solved" by legislators making treatment mandatory, regardless of ability or proof of ability to pay. This solution has, of course, just replaced a lot of rules with a new one.

A better approach is to develop a set of principles that anyone can sensibly apply. In the hospital example, for instance, such a new principle might have been to treat patients immediately who could be harmed by a delay. After such treatment was provided, the hospital could have determined whether it wished to offer more services that would be reasonably available elsewhere for those who could not pay. Surely, although this principle is clearly profit-minded, it is closer to what Jesus taught through the parable of the Good Samaritan than what some hospitals were previously doing.

We start with identifying principles to follow where great opportunities can be seized or large harm avoided. The Golden Rule (Matthew 7:12, NKJV) is a wonderful example of a principle that can properly guide at least some of an investigation center's conduct. Although we learned this principle from Jesus, similar principles can also be found in other faiths and even in some secular philosophies. This principle has its greatest value when we come into contact with visitors who are either unable or little able to tell us what help they need. Otherwise, the principle can best be applied by first determining what assistance someone would like to have, then considering what help would do the most good, subsequently examining yourself to see what you would want done in such circumstances, and finally checking your thinking with the person to be assisted to ensure its appropriateness before you act.

If you decide to embrace the Golden Rule as a guiding principle, your investigation center is likely to also require the application of some other principles to grasp more opportunities and avoid more harm. One such principle could be showing God's love to His children. Another possible principle could be to empower any three believing stakeholders to pray for guidance from the Holy Spirit and, after an appropriate delay to receive an answer from God, to act on whatever the majority learns should be done.

While I cannot hope to accurately present here what principles should be applied to your investigation center, I certainly encourage the use of any principles that the Bible commands. You should become familiar with all such principles so that they will spring more rapidly to mind when appropriate. Doing so will bless every part of your life.

Of potentially greater significance is directing all stakeholders to report any instances where great opportunities exist or the potential for substantial harm looms, and the center's approach does not seem adequate to deal with either one. I also recommend that you have those who make such reports suggest a principle that could be easily and accurately applied to deal with such circumstances.

In actually applying approved principles, you may find it helpful to provide some guidelines for what to do if two principles appear to be in conflict. One helpful approach for any such occurrence is to establish a hierarchy of principles. A principle that Jesus saw as universal, such as the Golden Rule, might be placed higher than a principle that is often applied in a narrow context, such as one related to keeping costs low. The conflict would be resolved in such a case by applying the principle that ranks higher on the center's value hierarchy.

As advocates for investigation centers, be sure to submit, as well, any ideas for principles to be added for comment by all stakeholders before making any changes. In this way, you can avoid many mistakes and much confusion.

Here's one final thought on this subject: Don't compel people to do anything they perceive is wrong. Otherwise, you will be undermining the moral foundation of the center. It's better to have a well-meant mistake occur than to make someone feel rotten about what he or she has done. Be sure to record any such instances of mistakes or moral compromises so that they can be studied to improve choices and applications of principles and procedures.

Building on this last observation, we now consider locating and adjusting practices that harm the morale of or cause concern among stakeholders. Here's an example of what can go wrong. On my last night in Malawi in 2014, my kind host convened a wonderful family dinner at one of the finest restaurants in Lilongwe. However, after dinner before anyone requested the check, our waiter unexpectedly arrived looking angry and began to complain about a fish dish that he claimed we had received and eaten. Quite aware of what we had consumed and with the remains in plain sight, we pointed out that we had received no fish dish. The waiter quickly responded that we had. A pointless debate continued for some time until one of the guests noticed a fish dish that sat untouched on the nearby table of some diners who had just left. We began to comprehend that a fish dish had been prepared, but this entree had been delivered to the wrong table. Pointing to the evidence just seemed to make the waiter angrier. A few minutes later, still not having received a check and not having seen the manager after requesting his presence, one of the guests went to the front desk to pay ... minus any charges for a fish dish. With the pleasant mood of the evening broken, all agreed that they would not return to the restaurant, and most said that they would tell others to do likewise.

While I was not able to investigate the cause of the problem, I suspect that the restaurant may have unintentionally contributed to our discomfort through its procedures. Here's one possibility: Some restaurants hold waiters strictly responsible for collecting money for any food that is prepared. In such cases, when the food leaves the kitchen, the waiter owns it until the diner pays. I don't know what the price of this particular dish was, but if it was similar to the others, the amount was close to being as large as the tip that a waiter could expect to receive from a party this size. If the restaurant held him responsible for that amount, the waiter would lose any financial benefit from having served us. If that was the case, I could easily appreciate why the waiter was upset.

Even if the waiter had been well trained to appease customers in all circumstances, it would be understandable for him to try to avoid taking a large personal loss as his first priority. Many times, leaders assume that stakeholders will do all the right things without much direction after such general principles are endorsed. As the Lilongwe restaurant example shows, leaders should, instead, expect the wrong things to be done on at least some occasions and be vigilant in seeking to locate problems when they happen and then to adjust the directions that are given until the right results almost always occur.

Having identified that a change is needed, we should now consider the value of and how to provide experiences with correctly applying any new principles, practices, or inspirational methods. The longer an investigation center has been operating and the more successful it has been, the more likely that stakeholders will find it hard to appreciate the advantages of and requirements for adding any improved principles, practices, or inspirational methods. It is just human nature to become complacent about or overly attached to the ways things have been done. Many people will humorously cite this observation in defense of a "no change" view: "If it ain't broke, don't fix it."

So what can be done? While many people lack the interest and imagination needed to appreciate and become excited about an improvement, almost anyone can be transformed by experiencing the superior results that are gained by applying one. In addition, most people appreciate the attention and respect they experience during a well-designed experience aimed at enhancing their effectiveness or providing them with more, or more desirable, benefits.

Let me outline for you the more important elements for people gaining such informative and revealing experiences so that you will more easily seek to duplicate them while providing experiences for correctly applying any new perspectives, practices, or inspirational methods to improve the investigation center:

- The people who lead the experience should be enthusiastic about the changes and have broad perspectives and deep insights concerning what has been previously done, and why and how improvements have been made.
- Conduct the experiences in a context that's highly relevant, interesting, and inspiring for those who are learning so that they will be easily able to see and deeply appreciate the reasons for the changes.
- Provide plenty of opportunities to mix with other people who have undergone or are undergoing the experiences so that their reactions can reinforce the learning and its significance.
- Show sincere and kind gratitude to those undergoing the new experiences, especially through some form of celebration.

- Check in from time to time with those who have had the experience to reinforce what has been learned and to provide additional evidence of its relevance.
- Ask for suggestions concerning how such experiences could be improved, as well as how participants could gain still more effectiveness.

Let's turn now to our last topic of this lesson: Monitor application of the new principles, practices, and inspirational methods, and make necessary adjustments in their use by changes or by providing better training. Accurately monitoring the effects of anything new presents several complex challenges.

First, many people will be inspired by the new initiative to do more than they have previously, based on believing the changes are helpful. These extra efforts can make the changes appear to be working better than they actually are, especially if the burst of added activity will not be sustained.

Second, the error rate while applying the changes will be initially higher than it will eventually be due to unavoidable confusion about what to do and delays in learning and skill development. As a result, the monitoring must pay special attention to whether the initial error rates are, indeed, dropping as they should.

Third, experience with the prior principles, practices, and inspirational methods will have created a set of expectations for what to measure and monitor in terms of the changes. Such expectations can lead us to use inappropriate measurements, blinding us to other perspectives, potential effects, and problems that are actually more important than the ones that we are accustomed to watching for. Any measurements should engage as many different stakeholders and perspectives as possible that can reveal something important about the most recent adjustments at the investigation center. In doing so, we must also search for better dimensions to measure, especially when new types of benefits are being provided, or new types of stakeholders are providing or receiving benefits.

If you do these things and listen to the Lord, your investigation center will just continue to grow in fruitfulness.

Thanks for your kind attention to *Investigation Centers*. I hope the material has blessed you. I will look forward to visiting your investigation center. Please invite me when you are ready by sending an e-mail (or your questions) to donmitchell@fastforward400.com/.

May God bless you, your family, and all you do in the name of Jesus!

Lesson Twenty-Seven Assignments

1. What principles could better direct stakeholders at your investigation center?

2. How should conflicts in applying these principles be handled?

3. How can you locate and eliminate practices that either reduce the morale of stakeholders or cause harm?

4. What experiences can you provide to stakeholders that will encourage them to make necessary changes in practices?

5. How will you measure the effectiveness of any improvements that are implemented?

Appendix A

Donald Mitchell's Testimony

He will lift you up.

Humble yourselves
in the sight of the Lord,
and He will lift you up.

— James 4:10 (NKJV)

Let me share with you how I became a Christian so you will know where I'm coming from with regard to encouraging you to become a Christian and to be fruitful in Godly contributions for creating and implementing breakthrough solutions.

There has been a long commitment to the Lord in our family. For example, I remember my great-grandmother, Edith Foster, reading the Bible every day. As a youngster, my mother regularly took me to Sunday school. It was my least favorite activity; sleeping was much preferred. I did enjoy listening to sermons, but it was frowned on to take youngsters to the adult services where the sermons were given.

If I pretended to be asleep, mom would sometimes let me stay in bed on Sundays. I was pretty good at pretending, and I soon was the biggest backslider in my Sunday school grade. Fortunately, it was an evangelical church so my classmates were always cooking up new schemes to get me to attend again. Because of my high opinion of myself, I would always return if invited to play my clarinet for the congregation.

By the time I turned thirteen, I was pretty full of myself. There wasn't much room for God in there alongside my exaggerated opinion of myself.

One day at home while my family was away for a drive, I felt really sick. By the time they returned, I was delirious. Within an hour, I was in the hospital where I would stay for two weeks as I barely survived a bad case of double pneumonia.

My physician, Dr. Helmsley, was a caring Christian and worried about my soul because my life was in jeopardy. He talked to me about our Heavenly Father, Jesus, and the Holy Spirit twice a day when he stopped by to check on me. During these conversations, I first learned how to become a Christian through being born again. I also came to realize that I couldn't stop sinning on my own. I needed a Savior, Jesus Christ! After I recovered, he took my mom and me to a tent revival meeting.

Having recovered from the illness, I soon pushed God out of my life again. During the next year, I was, instead, very caught up in athletics. When I was in ninth grade, I desperately wanted to make a contribution to our junior high track team, which had an unlikely chance of winning the big meet. Our coach, Mr. Layman, told each of us exactly what had to be accomplished for the team to win. I was determined to do my part. I had to come in first!

But that was not likely to happen. Based on past performances, there were at least two people who could out leap me in the standing broad jump, my main event. To make such a jump, you stand on a slightly raised, forward-tilted board and spring outward as far as you can into a sand-filled pit. After two of the three jumping rounds, I knew it was hopeless. I was in sixth place and four of the competitors' jumps were longer than I had ever gone before. I also didn't like the board we were using.

Remembering that we should call on God when we need help, I thought of praying ... but what I wanted seemed so unimportant in God's terms that I didn't think it was worthy of prayer. So I decided to make God an offer instead: "Dear God, help me win this event, and I'm yours forever." After all, if He came through, any doubts I had about God would be dispelled.

I stepped onto the broad-jump board and felt very calm. I did my routine and took off into the air. Instantly, I felt light as a feather cradled in a large, gentle hand that was lifting me up. I was dropped softly at the far end of the pit. I had outleapt everyone and gone more than six inches past my best previous jump. I couldn't believe it. Then I remembered my promise to God, thanked Him, repented my sins, accepted Jesus as my Lord and Savior, and ran off to tell everyone on the team.

Even more remarkable, I was the only person on the team who performed up to the plan. Knowing what had to be done had probably given us performance anxiety, and athletes underperformed because they didn't believe they could do what the team needed. I also suspect that God wanted to make a point with me that I needed Him.

Within a few days, I started to think that perhaps I'd just developed a new broad-jump technique and God didn't have a role at all. God soon dispelled that thought by making sure that my jumps for the rest of my life were much shorter than I had jumped when He lifted me up.

Since then, God has been regularly speaking to me through the Holy Spirit. I have learned to pay attention and to act promptly. When I pursue my own ideas, things don't go so well. When I follow His directions, things work out great. That's my secret to high performance, and I just wanted to share it with you so you could benefit, too. He knows the answers, even when you and I don't ... which is most of the time.

As a management consultant, the Holy Spirit has often filled me with knowledge about what the consequences of one set of actions would be compared to another for my clients. Naturally, I always recommended as the Holy Spirit directed me. Clients often told me that they were impressed by how certain I was of my conclusions and of how persuasive I could be in describing the advantages of whatever recommendations were made. Once again, the explanatory words came from the Holy Spirit, rather than from me.

Unfortunately, I wasn't comfortable in my younger days sharing my faith with clients, and I wrongly gave many people the impression that I was the author of the solutions rather than merely the transmitter.

I wish I had been more faithful in this regard. I apologize to my clients for having missed so many great witnessing opportunities. I didn't always listen as well as I should in making decisions that primarily affected me, but God would always do something to get my attention. Here is an example. I made an investment that I hoped would reduce my taxes in addition to making some money. I didn't have a good feeling from the Holy Spirit at the time, and I shouldn't have invested.

My tax return was later audited by the Internal Revenue Service concerning that investment. It turned out I was in the wrong for the deductions I had taken. Anticipating a big tax bill plus penalties and interest, you can imagine my astonishment when the revised tax return showed me owing no additional money to the government, even though I had lost on the audit issues. I knew that result was a gift from God, and I was overwhelmed by His wisdom and power in protecting me. Praise God for His mercy!

I rededicated my life to Jesus in 1995, and I have enjoyed great peace since then. I have also done a lot better in being obedient to the Holy Spirit and to what the Bible tells us to do in all aspects of my life. Many blessings have been mine since then.

After being directed by God to start The 400 Year Project (to demonstrate how everyone in the world could make improvements 20-times faster and more effectively than normal with no additional resources) in 1995, I continued to receive His instructions. In 2005, for example, God told me to start explaining to people how to live their lives by gaining more joy from what they already have.

In the summer of 2006, I began to see how The 400 Year Project could be brought to a successful conclusion (as I reported in *Adventures of an Optimist*, Mitchell and Company Press, 2007). Realizing that perhaps I had devoted too much of my attention to this one challenge, I began to seek ways to rebalance my life. One of those rebalancing methods was to spend more time communing with God through prayer, Scriptural studies, attending church services and Bible classes, and listening more to the still, small voice within.

For several years I had been enjoying the devotionals sent to me daily over the Internet by evangelist Bill Keller. One of those devotionals pierced me like an arrow that summer. The evangelist reminded his readers that our responsibility as believers is to share our faith with others through our example and sharing the Gospel message from the Bible. Not feeling well equipped to do more than try to be a good example, I began to pray about what else I should be doing.

The next day, my answer came: I was to launch a global contest to locate the most effective ways that souls were being saved and be sure that information was shared widely. This sharing would be a blessing for those who wished to fulfill the Great Commission to spread the Good News of Jesus as commanded in Matthew 28:18-20 (NKJV):

And Jesus came and spoke to them, saying, "All authority has been given to Me in heaven and on earth. Go therefore and make disciples of all the nations, baptizing them in the name of the Father and of the Son and of the Holy Spirit, teaching them to observe all things that I have commanded you; and lo, I am with you always, *even* to the end of the age."

The contest winners were Jubilee Worship Center in Hobart, Indiana, and Step by Step Ministries in Porter, Indiana. You can read their experiences to learn amazingly effective ways to help unsaved people choose to accept Salvation in *Witnessing Made Easy: Yes, You Can Make a Difference* (Jubilee Worship Center Step by Step Press, 2010) by Bishop Dale P. Combs, Lisa Combs, Jim Barbarossa, Carla Barbarossa, and me. Six other worthy ideas and practices from the contest for assisting more people in learning about and some to be moved by the Holy Spirit to pledge their lives to Jesus are described in a second book, *Ways You Can Witness: How the Lost Are Found* (Salvation Press, 2010) by Cherie Hill, Roger de Brabant, Drew Dickens, Gael Torcise, Wendy Lobos, Herpha Jane Obod, Gisele Umugiraneza, and me.

Let me tell you another interesting thing about my life with Jesus. When my daughter was about a year old, I suffered what resembled a stroke that caused me to start to become paralyzed. As I could feel my face's muscles freezing, I immediately prayed to Jesus to stop the paralysis and He did. I was left with a lot of pain and numbness on the left side of my body and was very weak for over a year.

Part of that pain continued for the next twenty-two years until, on November 8, 2009, I asked two of my pastors during a communion service to pray in the name of Jesus that the remaining pain be removed. During the prayer, the pain started leaving immediately and was totally gone within a half hour. As I felt the pain leaving me, through some power traveling inch by inch down my body, I was overcome with gratitude and fell on my knees in thanks.

That wasn't the only time He recently healed me. Encouraged by that miraculous experience, I came forward again on December 19, 2010, during another communion service to request prayer for relief from the pain in my wrists that was making it difficult for me to write books to serve Him and to do my other work. Knowing that my mother had been plagued with arthritis, I assumed it was a similar onset for me. My pastors were occupied with prayers for other members of the congregation. This time an elder of the church and his wife anointed me with oil and prayed for me. Almost immediately, my whole body shook violently in a way that I couldn't stop. Gradually, the shaking was reduced until it ceased after about half an hour, and my wrist pain was totally gone. It has not returned. I was even more overwhelmed that He had healed me again. Can anyone appreciate all the goodness that God has in store for us?

Let me share yet another miraculous healing (not the last that I've experienced). I've always been troubled with many respiratory and food allergies and sensitivities. In my sixties, these problems had become worse. I finally reached the point where it was difficult to be in the same room with other people due to my reactions to any deodorants and scents they had applied. During still another communion service on January 16, 2012, two pastors again prayed for me to be relieved of these problems so that I could be a better witness for Him. Once again, power filled my body. My allergies and sensitivities were gone in a few minutes. Since then, I have had no recurrences of the problems. It has made a huge improvement in my life and in my witnessing.

I have also been saved by God from what I believed to be certain death on twelve occasions, most recently on July 2, 2013. I won't go into all of these events, but I did want you to be aware that He is always touching all aspects of my life in beneficial ways.

While it's up to God to decide if and when He wants to heal us or to protect us from harm, it's certainly reassuring to know that He has the ability and power to do anything He wants.

Glory be to God! Praise Him always! His miracles, grace, and mercy never end. I am so happy and honored to be His servant and witness to you.

Appendix B

Summary of
The 400 Year Project

Therefore we also pray always for you
that our God would count you worthy of this calling,
and fulfill all the good pleasure of His goodness
and the work of faith with power,
that the name of our Lord Jesus Christ
may be glorified in you, and you in Him,
according to the grace of our God
and the Lord Jesus Christ.

— 2 Thessalonians 1:11-12 (NKJV)

One morning during the summer of 1995 at around 3:45 a.m., I felt a warm presence fill the bedroom. In response, my body temperature seemed to rise and I felt deliriously happy. A voice that I didn't recognize filled my mind and told me in tones that were more resonant and powerful than James Earl Jones on his best day that I should hold a meeting on the autumnal equinox for all of my management consulting clients to share and celebrate their greatest accomplishments. At the end of the meeting, I should announce that I would be starting a 20-year project to find ways for the whole world to make 400 years of normal progress in only 20 years, beginning in 2015 and finishing in 2035. For the next few weeks, I could think of little else.

What had happened? I prayed over the experience quite a bit and concluded that God had sent me a message. Why me? I have no idea. Maybe He couldn't find anyone else crazy enough to take on such an impossible task. I certainly felt that only God would know how to do it.

Why that time frame? I don't know, but it later occurred to me that the 2000th anniversary of Jesus' resurrection would occur during 2015–2035. Perhaps that was an important connection. Since then, I've come to appreciate that 20 is a spiritually important number to God: Notice that the dimensions of the Holy of Holies in the Temple were measured in terms of 20 cubits. But who knows, except God?

How would I pursue this project? I had no idea, not even a clue. All I knew was that I was supposed to make this announcement at the autumnal equinox.

I quickly organized the meeting. Clients graciously agreed to fly in to share their triumphs and lessons with one another. Not knowing how anyone else would take the announcement of this new project, I decided to keep it to myself. I also had the impression that I should keep the project private until the announcement. Otherwise, why make the announcement then rather than sooner?

The event went much better than I could have hoped, especially since I wasn't sure what to say during the unexpected announcement. Almost all listeners were encouraging, and many volunteered to help with the project.

A key early focus was to engage in writing a book that Peter Drucker, the founder of the management discipline, had encouraged Carol Coles and me to write encapsulating a problem-solving method that we had been using for many years. We were fortunate to gain the assistance of Robert Metz, a veteran author and journalist, as a coauthor to lead us through the publication twists and turns. That book was *The 2,000 Percent Solution*, still the most widely read publication produced by The 400 Year Project.

Having experienced a warm reception for this book, I was delighted when the Holy Spirit kept providing concepts, processes, or the actual words for many future books, of which nineteen more have been completed with the publication of *Investigation Centers*. Through applying these books, readers and students of mine have created their own breakthroughs by employing The 400 Year Project's methods. I'm aware of successful demonstration projects that have been conducted so far in over 60 countries. There are probably more such successes that I'm unaware of. What a blessing this has been! Praise God!

I have also had the pleasure of conducting several global contests, building experience to supplement the concepts first articulated in *The Ultimate Competitive Advantage* about this way of making rapid advances.

I also established a learning organization, The Billionaire Entrepreneurs' Master Mind, to advance how complementary 2,000 percent solutions could be most effectively developed and combined. I continue to be delighted by the lessons developed by that group, which have richly informed *Business Basics* and the three books in the recently completed Advanced Business series.

Today, The 400 Year Project is ready for prime time. The books, experiences, and networks of breakthrough problem solvers provide a sound foundation for expanding and transforming God's Kingdom in every possible dimension between now and 2035 by far more than 20 times. I am delighted that you will be part of creating such remarkable transformations.

May God bless you, your family, and all you do in the name of Jesus!

www.ingramcontent.com/pod-product-compliance
Lightning Source LLC
Chambersburg PA
CBHW070952040426
42443CB00007B/469